How to Offer Effective Wellbeing Support to Law Students

For Mum, Dad, Adam, Maya, Everett and Elspeth

How to Offer Effective Wellbeing Support to Law Students

Edited by

Lydia Katherine Bleasdale

Professor of Legal Education, School of Law, University of Leeds, UK

Edward Elgar PUBLISHING

Cheltenham, UK • Northampton, MA, USA

© The Editor and Contributing Authors Severally 2024

All rights reserved. No part of this publication may be reproduced, stored in a retrieval system or transmitted in any form or by any means, electronic, mechanical or photocopying, recording, or otherwise without the prior permission of the publisher.

Published by
Edward Elgar Publishing Limited
The Lypiatts
15 Lansdown Road
Cheltenham
Glos GL50 2JA
UK

Edward Elgar Publishing, Inc.
William Pratt House
9 Dewey Court
Northampton
Massachusetts 01060
USA

A catalogue record for this book
is available from the British Library

Library of Congress Control Number: 2023952682

This book is available electronically in the **Elgar**online
Law subject collection
http://dx.doi.org/10.4337/9781803920801

ISBN 978 1 80392 079 5 (cased)
ISBN 978 1 80392 080 1 (eBook)

Printed and bound by CPI Group (UK) Ltd, Croydon, CR0 4YY

Contents

	List of contributors	vii
1	Introduction to *How to Offer Effective Wellbeing Support to Law Students* Lydia Bleasdale	1
2	Navigating a student support leadership role as an early career academic: supporting yourself to better support others Rachael O'Connor	5
3	Looking back to look forward: scaffolding the student support pathway for students through the eyes of an early career legal academic Laura Hughes-Gerber, Noel McGuirk, Rafael Savva	24
4	Pastoral support: student views Georgina May Collins	39
5	Supporting law students: student support officers' perspectives Lydia Bleasdale, Max Broady, Charlotte Guest, James Johnston	59
6	Reflections on the influence of staff and student sex and gender on the provision of pastoral support Jenny Gibbons	74
7	How to offer effective pastoral support in a distance learning institution Liz Hardie, Francine Ryan	88
8	You see me, but can you hear me? Let's talk about race Iwi Ugiagbe-Green	102
9	Wellbeing in the classroom Georgina May Collins, Rita D'Alton-Harrison, David Yuratich	120
10	Integrating wellbeing into the law school curriculum Emma Jones	140

| 11 | Being a personal tutor in a diverse HE sector
Vicky Martin | 157 |

Index 172

Contributors

Lydia Bleasdale, Professor, School of Law, University of Leeds, UK

Max Broady, Student Support Manager, University of Leeds, UK

Georgina May Collins, Lecturer in Law, Lancaster University, UK

Rita D'Alton-Harrison, Professor, Royal Holloway, University of London, UK

Jenny Gibbons, Subject Head, Kaplan, UK

Charlotte Guest, Project Officer, University of Leeds, UK

Liz Hardie, Senior Lecturer, School of Law, The Open University, UK

Laura Hughes-Gerber, Lecturer in Law, Lancaster University, UK

James Johnston, Programme Support Team Leader, University of Leeds, UK

Emma Jones, Senior Lecturer, School of Law, University of Sheffield, UK

Vicky Martin, Senior Lecturer, School of Law, Manchester Metropolitan University, UK

Noel McGuirk, Lecturer in Law, Lancaster University, UK

Rachael O'Connor, Associate Professor and Trustee of LawCare, School of Law, University of Leeds, UK

Francine Ryan, Senior Lecturer, School of Law, The Open University, UK

Rafael Savva, Lecturer in Law, Lancaster University, UK

Iwi Ugiagbe-Green, Reader, Manchester Metropolitan Business School, UK

David Yuratich, Senior Lecturer in Law, University of Exeter, UK

1. Introduction to *How to Offer Effective Wellbeing Support to Law Students*

Lydia Bleasdale

When I was a first year Law student, I struggled hugely. I didn't want to be a lawyer, I hated the subjects I was studying, and I felt I had nobody to talk to. In contrast, everyone seemed to be having a great time and to understand what was going on in our modules. I entered my second year with a relatively low average and a determination to leave the course if I couldn't get a mark I was happy with in a particular first semester module. That module was taught by my favourite lecturer: funny, clear, knew his subject inside out. He was also my new personal tutor: I had been allocated to him after my previous tutor – who I met briefly, once, when they were late for a group meeting in the first few weeks of term – left the University. I did get a mark I was happy with in that second year module, I started to 'find my people,' and I was able to focus more on the topics I was most interested in. Over the next two years, that lecturer nurtured me through the degree and showed me how to be the type of academic I would want every student to experience – without him, I wouldn't be here, and wouldn't be doing what I do.

I don't always get student support right, and there can be structural challenges which make achieving what we want more difficult. The hope is that this book will serve as a useful starting point for considering how to 'do' student support, particularly if it's a role you're new to. It has been written to increase your confidence in supporting students, albeit with a firm focus on knowing the limits of your role and abilities. As tutors supporting students, we cannot fix systemic, structural issues inherent within our workplaces, or within broader support services such as the NHS, but the book will give you insights into how you can proactively support students, in combination with professional services colleagues, within the classroom, on campus and online, and within the broader curriculum. You'll be encouraged to view student support as something which 'takes a village' (you should feel able to ask for help and to work alongside others, whether that's in finding the information you need or in providing support to the students); to reflect upon work-life balance and how you might manage this while also effectively supporting your students; and to put yourself into hypothetical situations where you can reflect upon what you might do if faced with similar issues. I hope this text will act as confirmation of what you're already doing well, as well as giving you some new ideas and perspectives.

As well as telling you what the text will do, I think it's just as important to be clear about what it does NOT do. It does not, for example, offer 'mental health training' or 'personal tutor training,' not least because the authors would not regard themselves as qualified to provide that. Indeed, a common theme running throughout the text is the need to know the boundaries of your role, training and expertise, and to recognise that a core part of your role – as a personal tutor, or as a tutor on a programme of study more generally – is to understand your institution's processes and policies, and the opportunities which exist to refer to experts who can help with e.g. counselling. The expectations placed on you as far as supporting the wellbeing of your students is concerned will vary by institution – potentially quite drastically – and hopefully this text will give you some insight into how to manage those expectations.

The text doesn't cover every type of student you might encounter: doing so would be an impossible task within the word limit! It does, however, reference some specific students, such as those who are care experienced, international students, commuter students, students with disabilities, and students who are otherwise underrepresented and/or minoritised. It doesn't explicitly cover postgraduate students, although much of what is written could be equally applicable to their experiences, and the experiences of staff working with them. Most of the focus is on students who are taught on campus, although see Chapter seven for a discussion of teaching remotely in the context of the Open University.

At the start of this process, I envisaged the book providing a single definition of 'wellbeing,' 'wellness,' and 'pastoral support' which could be used consistently throughout the text. As the chapters started to roll in, though, I took the view that would be an artificial exercise, particularly as the text is partly designed to give you insight into the authors' differing perspectives on student support. The text displays the variety of approaches you can take to those topics, and the variety of approaches you'll see taken throughout your time supporting the wellbeing of students.

There are other areas where there is no agreed approach. At first glance, this might make it appear as if there are inconsistencies within the text, but again this merely reflects the diversity of views you're already encountering, or will encounter, within your working life. The approach taken to 'personal tutoring' across institutions varies a huge amount, which is reflected in the advice offered by the authors. Whether 'imposter syndrome' warrants focus on the individual, the institution, or a mixture of both is an emerging issue which certainly gave me pause for thought. Similarly, the language we use to describe students who are the first in their families to attend university is contentious, with people with experience of being in that position not necessarily agreeing on whether 'non-traditional' is a better description than 'underrepresented' or 'first generation.'

That being said, there are clear themes which emerge from the text (which aren't necessarily specific to law students), as identified by the authors themselves. The importance of a sense of belonging and a sense of community to student support and wellbeing is discussed in numerous chapters, alongside the importance of staff community and wellbeing: it can be more challenging to demonstrate compassion, approachability or kindness, and to actively listen, if we ourselves feel like we don't belong, or aren't able to practise self-care as much as we might like. Some authors reflect on the effect of the pandemic in bringing these issues to the fore, both for students and for staff: there has been a (sometimes welcome) impetus for change in terms of teaching methods, for example, but that has come at a time when both staff and students have felt on unsteady ground and unsure of their own capabilities. Those experiences have not been felt to the same extent by everyone, owning to the diversity of the student body: authors emphasise the need to adopt a personalised approach as far as possible, one which recognises the individuality of students in everything we do. An inclusive approach to student support, teaching and assessment is necessary, recognising the prevalence of protected characteristics as well as the generic experiences of Law students as a whole.

This ties in with another common theme: student wellbeing support isn't just something that happens in 1-2-1 tutee meetings, or on the basis of a 'deficit' model (whereby students are supported only after something 'goes wrong'): it can be integrated within inclusive teaching and assessment design, and the broader curriculum. Chapters nine and ten cover specific ways in which this might be done within the classroom and through the broader curriculum, while others consider how student support can be integrated through sharing vulnerabilities (see Chapter two, for example); proactively recognising and addressing the role race plays in classroom interactions (Chapter eight); and recognising the individuality of students (see Chapters three, four, and eleven, for example).

The text also encourages you to consider how you might draw upon other support and expertise, such as through collaboration with student support colleagues (Chapter five, for example), and by recognising the limits of what you can achieve within the time available. This is critical for anyone supporting students, but particularly those who are most likely to experience the heaviest teaching workload, bringing them into contact with the largest number of students (see Chapter six for a discussion of why this can make the workload associated with student support a gendered issue).

Like good student support, editing a book takes a village. My thanks go to the authors for their varied and insightful perspectives and advice on successfully supporting students, and to Stephanie Tytherleigh as commissioning editor: their collective diligence, professionalism, expertise and enthusiasm has made them all a joy to work with. I owe particular thanks to Michael Doherty, Verona Ní Drisceoil and Ishan Kolhatkar for always being there (with bad jokes, in Ish's case); to Imogen Jones for her friendship in and out of work (I'll forgive you the chocolate orange); to Emma Flint; to the entire Connecting Legal Education community; and to my students for making me a better – but by no means perfect – tutor and colleague.

Professor Alastair Mullis: thank you for giving me the push and the support I needed to reach my potential as a colleague on a Teaching and Scholarship contract. You were the Head of School I needed and wanted, and I will be forever grateful for what you did for me and for the wider Leeds community.

Finally, to return to where this Introduction began: thank you, Professor Nick Taylor, for all the advice, reassurance, laughs and wine over the past 20 years, and for encouraging me to stay on the Law course (even if it did mean you kept another scouser around). Without you, this book and my career wouldn't exist.

2. Navigating a student support leadership role as an early career academic: supporting yourself to better support others

Rachael O'Connor

2.1 INTRODUCTION

The hope of this chapter is that whilst reading it, you reflect on things you have done and achieved so far as an early career academic in the student support space and celebrate your wins, however insignificant they may feel. If you are someone like me who has fallen victim to the falsehood of 'impostor syndrome', you may think you're not achieving much by comparison to those around you. It's important to take stock every now and again. The chapter also hopes to support you in reflecting on where challenges exist in your current student support leadership role, or to anticipate challenges that may arise in future roles, and how you might improve your practice for the benefit of others and yourself. The chapter therefore provides some reflections and practical tips based on my experiences, recognising how closely intertwined student wellbeing and staff wellbeing are[1].

Firstly, I want to tell you who I am so you can understand my positionality and thereby judge my credibility for yourself. I have been an academic for five years in a Russell Group law school where I was previously a joint honours undergraduate student. I identify as feeling under-represented in academia as I am a first-generation student and academic from a working-class background.

---

[1] See e.g., Chris Wilson et al., 'Curriculum design for mental health and wellbeing: guidance and resources for learning and teaching development programmes in higher education' (2022, Advance HE), 25–71 (Theme 1); Liz Brewster et al., 'Look after the staff and they would look after the students' cultures of wellbeing and mental health in the university setting' (2021), Journal of Further and Higher Education, 4; Richard Collier, 'Blackstones Tower Revisited: Legal Academic Wellbeing, Marketization and the Post-Pandemic Law School', *Amicus Curiae*, Series 2, Spring 2021, 2(3), 477.

It's something I'm fiercely proud of but also an identity that has triggered various internal conflicts during my career. I was a corporate tax lawyer in an international law firm before coming into academia. In my former corporate life, I became conditioned towards the belief that wellbeing was 'nice to have if workload allowed' and that more work = more billings = good.[2] My growing sense of 'un-belonging' in that corporate world and its conflict with my personal identity and values led me to a change quite early in my legal career to become an academic. After almost two years of lecturing on a teaching and scholarship focussed contract,[3] I began a student support leadership role in my school in summer 2020 during the height of the COVID-19 pandemic and the transition to fully online learning and support. Being thrust into a leadership role during a time of such uncertainty sent my feelings of what I assumed then to be 'impostor syndrome' spiralling even further:[4] 'I really shouldn't have applied for this role, I have no idea what I'm doing', I told myself repeatedly. However, three years on, I'm still here, finding my own style and growing in confidence and now have a university-level leadership role. Although I still have much to learn and more confidence to grow, I can now appreciate what I bring to these roles, despite initial hang-ups and self-doubt around being relatively junior and described by others as 'non-traditional'.[5]

I hope there is at least one thing that resonates with you in this chapter and that you get some sense of comfort in solidarity, as well as at least one thing you can take forward and use in your own practice of student support leadership, whether current or in the future. The chapter is broken down into sub-sections, drawing mostly on my collaborative work with students who also identify as under-represented and encouraging readers to think about how you can do more in your roles collaboratively with students.

The first section reflects on the importance of taking care of ourselves and not just telling others to do so. With experience of the commercial legal sector and academia, I have felt many frustrations encountering meaningless

---

[2] See e.g. LawCare, 'Life in the Law 2020/21' (2021) 'It's time for legal workplaces to accept that long hours, heavy workloads, poor work-life balance and the lack of effective supervision is undermining wellbeing' 80, available at: lawcare.org.uk/media/14vhquzz/lawcare-lifeinthelaw-v6-final.pdf (accessed 2 October 2023).

[3] Lydia Bleasdale, 'Examining Teaching-Focused Law Teachers Through the Prism of Self-Determination Theory' in Caroline Strevens and Emma Jones, *Wellbeing and the Legal Academy* (Springer, 2023).

[4] On student experiences of 'impostor syndrome', see Chapter 11.

[5] See Rachael O'Connor, 'Challenging the "traditional": how "micro-communities" can bring about big change', available at: spotlight.leeds.ac.uk/world-changers/challenging-the-traditional/index.html (accessed 2 October 2023).

corporate jargon about wellbeing,[6] so I hope you will find what I discuss comes from a genuine place of sharing things that have helped me. The second and third sections focus on relationships and the importance of providing support to colleagues and building your own networks of people who value similar things to you and can offer new perspectives, as well as people who lift you up. The fourth section explores 'unhealthy hierarchies' in academia and how we can contribute to breaking them down to create cultures where we can thrive and thereby do better for our students, with our students. The chapter closes with reflections on being our authentic selves in student support leadership, a potentially impactful tool for challenging cultures within institutions which breed impostor phenomenon.[7] Whilst the chapter finishes with my top tips for managing student support leadership roles, I hope you will draw your own personalised messages from it, based on who you are, where you are and what your role is (or future roles you plan to undertake), because just as there is no one student experience or voice, there is also no one staff experience or voice. We learn from sharing our experiences and voices, so here's mine …

2.2 WHAT ADVICE WOULD YOU GIVE TO A STUDENT IN YOUR SHOES? THE ART OF PRACTICING WHAT WE PREACH

I have often struggled with feelings of guilt and personal responsibility for individual students and student 'groups'. Trying to solve everything for everyone[8] inevitably leads to overworking, neglecting other areas of the job (often those more crucial to progression), and feeling like you're not getting anywhere because your remit is too broad or unattainable. For example, tackling awarding gaps, making personal tutoring student led, supporting students who join university through 'widening participation' schemes,[9] addressing the upsurge in mental health issues since the pandemic[10] and ensuring everything

---

[6] Anecdotal but I once read in a law firm's wellbeing handbook something along the lines of: 'if you start having negative thoughts, just ignore them and think about something else'.

[7] See Terri Simpkins, 'It's Not A Bloody Syndrome', available at: linkedin.com/pulse/its-bldy-syndrome-mythbusting-imposter-phenomenon-terri-simpkin/ (accessed 19 October 2023). See also Chapter 11 on the importance of being our authentic selves as personal tutors.

[8] See also Chapter 5.

[9] See Stacey Mottershaw, 'Why we need to stop using the term widening participation', available at: hepi.ac.uk/2021/12/17/why-we-need-to-stop-using-the-term-widening-participation/ (accessed 2 October 2023).

[10] See e.g. Student Minds, 'Student Mental Health: Life in a Pandemic Research Wave III' (January 2022), available at: studentminds.org.uk/uploads/3/7/8/4/3784584/student_minds_research_wave_iii__2_.pdf (accessed 2 October 2023).

is 'evidence based'[11] are just some examples of a seemingly endless to-do list that might fall within a student support leadership role. It won't surprise you that I often feel a particular affinity with students from similar backgrounds to mine and a responsibility to ensure they have appropriate support structures and spaces to be their authentic selves, to challenge barriers that I never got the opportunity to as a student.[12] I also have the additional burden in this space of being a woman. We know, typically, pastoral work falls more heavily on female colleagues.[13] Consequently, there are significant wellbeing risks to taking on a role like mine which I hadn't appreciated beforehand.

Furthermore, as I started to work with students from different under-represented backgrounds such as when supporting international students with transitioning (not assimilating[14]) to life in the UK,[15] issues and barriers associated with intersectional identity characteristics arose such as race, ethnicity, faith and sexuality. As I learn more about students and the vast array of challenges they may face in trying to become part of their university community and get their degree, the desire and pressure to try and 'solve' those challenges increases. There is always more to be done, always another statistic to try and change to prove your value to your school or university. This is when we can fall into the trap of 'throwing the kitchen sink' at student support (and I have), trying to do everything at once for all students, or feeling like we have a duty to be the 'saviour' or infallible role model of outstanding student support. That pressure can become overwhelming and is unsustainable.

There are no easy answers to shutting off these feelings but here, I share with you what has supported me to better support myself and consequently, colleagues and students. We spend so much time advising students about taking care of themselves, how to be more efficient, the importance of communicating and not suffering in silence etc. How often do we give ourselves this advice? How can we engage in authentic supportive relationships with students and colleagues if we don't practice what we preach ourselves?

---

[11] I don't personally believe in this all the time – if we don't sometimes just 'give it a go', we can perpetuate the same problems and barriers.
[12] See also Chapter 6.
[13] See e.g., Brewster et al, (n 1). See also Chapter 6.
[14] See e.g., Victor Thomas et al, 'Leveraging Common Ground: Improving International and Domestic Students' Interaction Through Mutual Engagement' (2018) 8(3) Journal of International Students 1386–97.
[15] See also Chapter 5.

2.2.1 Teamwork Actually Does Make the Dream Work

It sounds cliché but it's so often true. Avoid reinventing the wheel if possible.[16] It can feel like there is a continual pressure to innovate and do things differently and it can be hard to know where to focus. I have found it particularly important to collaborate with professional services colleagues working in student support and with students, rather than trying to do everything myself.[17] Academia often felt quite isolating and lonely when I first joined after being used to teamwork as a lawyer. In my first few years as a lecturer, I got used to doing everything by myself. Since taking on this leadership role, I have needed to work much more collegially, proactively catching up with other colleagues working in student support and related areas, even if we're not directly working together – student support permeates and overlaps with almost everything e.g. assessment, diversity and inclusion work, academic integrity, student futures etc. Whilst that was hard to readjust to, it has become an important source of balance and sanity: sharing ideas with colleagues, working on plans together, delivering initiatives as a team. This interdisciplinary approach to supporting students enables me to see a broader picture and consider a range of opinions, becoming more empathetic with diverse perspectives and ways of working, rather than just my own narrow positionality which, although under-represented, is just one view. This translates into my interactions with students and has inspired me to work much more collaboratively with them, as explored later. It also gives me insight into the resources and ideas that exist within my school and university which we can learn from, adapt and develop, potentially reaching transdisciplinary solutions to common challenges. Just as we encourage students to seek support and build positive relationships with peers,[18] it's important that we do the same, otherwise leadership as a junior colleague may feel like a pretty lonely place.

2.2.2 What Makes You, 'You'?

Whilst my job is extremely important to me, the last few years during the COVID-19 pandemic have starkly reminded me how important all aspects of my life are, of which my career is only part. When working in a student facing role, it's easy to always be 'on call' and for other aspects of life to always come second (or third, or fourth ...). I hope you won't roll your eyes too hard reading

---

[16] See also Chapter 9, discussing embedding wellbeing into the curriculum.
[17] On time and wellbeing implications of student support for staff, see also Chapter 4; on the importance of conversations between academic and professional services colleagues, see also Chapter 5.
[18] On peer mentoring as a support tool, see also Chapter 7.

this in light of what I said above about corporate wellbeing jargon, but I want to acknowledge the importance of holding on to doing things you love that make you 'you', even when your role becomes busy and/or stressful. I believe particularly as early career colleagues, it's important to fight to make this possible even if we sometimes fail, otherwise we are perpetuating the unhealthy environments academia (and particularly law) are renowned for.[19] I discuss this from a particular angle – whilst I am a committed dog mother, I don't have human children or other family members to care for currently (although I have had caring responsibilities previously). I currently have a permanent employment contract and work in a financially stable university. I recognise how much of a difference these privileges make to the ability to do what I am talking about.

However, no matter who we are, we have likely all been impacted by the endless meetings we get invited to as a result of having oversight of an area, despite the meetings not always being relevant, the feeling of needing to keep up with 'academic social media', the eternally pinging e-mail inbox … sometimes, we have to actively say no to these things and instead, do things that fill up our cup again. For me, it's CrossFit training and performing in community musical theatre (a random but joyful combination). Whatever your 'thing' is, try to hold on to it and prioritise it, as much as you do your work. Make that hobby or passion part of your 'goals' or 'to do list' every week, alongside work.[20] This is probably my best example of 'practice what you preach' because I'm always telling students to make sure they keep up with their hobbies or find new ones at university after continually seeing students 'give up' things they love when they start their degree because of workload concerns. I talk to them regularly about my hobbies to remind them that they are more than 'just a law student'. Whilst this primarily contributes to building authentic connections with my students, it also does me good to remember I am more than 'just my job'.

Is there anything you've stopped doing since you started your role or that's becoming difficult to fit in? What could support you in getting back to it? I won't give you any advice on how to do that, given what I've noted above about my environment and life but a very small thing that has supported me is saying 'no' more. For example, saying no to lunchtime or end of day meetings

---

[19] See LawCare (n 2).
[20] See the Serious Leisure podcast for some inspiration, particularly 'Why Leisure Matters' (to better understand the concept of 'serious leisure' and its positive impact on wellbeing); and 'COVID19 pandemic resilience' and the value of prioritising our sustained hobbies for the often elusive 'work/life balance', available at: seriousleisure.podbean.com/ (accessed 2 October 2023). I recorded my own episode in June 2023 so keep an ear out! On the importance of self-care in student support, see Chapter 10.

if they're not urgent and asking for a different time where possible. Saying no to joining meetings/forums/committees where I know my work and input isn't central and I'm unlikely to contribute. Also turning e-mail and Teams notifications off on my phone so that my evenings and weekends are generally kept work free (except maybe in marking season …). I return to my point above in saying this – we are all different, so we have to do what works for us. The point I want to stress is to give time to thinking about what works and doesn't work for you and make a change/say no if your list comes out with several things that are damaging your wellbeing and/or enjoyment of your job.

2.2.3 Putting Compassion into Policy

As we become involved in student support at strategic levels, we can get bogged down in data, policies and procedures and forget the human side of leadership which, in my view, is vital to its success. We can't have one without the other, just as we wouldn't advise students to follow instructions without considering them in their own context. When I first started getting involved in university policies and decision making, I felt compelled to follow rules to the letter. However, I believe it is an important part of our role as student support leaders to inject humanity and compassion into policies.[21] This is how I've often managed to make peace with myself over difficult decisions. This isn't about finding loopholes in policies or showing bias. It's about the basic act of being human when it comes to academic procedures such as fitness to study or progression meetings. Outcomes might not always feel fair, for example, if a student has missed a deadline by five minutes – this can be hard to deal with and feelings of guilt start to creep in. I might not always make decisions which are ideal for every student. However, if decisions I make have been discussed with trusted colleagues in appropriate forums and/or consulted on with students where possible and appropriate, I know those decisions are the right ones, driven by an empathetic desire to do the best by our students.

---

[21] See Bridgette Bewick, 'Why do we need a compassionate campus? And how do we get there?', available at: spotlight.leeds.ac.uk/world-changers/compassionate-campus/index.html (accessed 2 October 2023). See also Theo Gilbert, 'Compassion's gaze in the University curriculum' on compassion in the classroom to catalyse peer inclusivity, available at: researchgate.net/publication/318921562_The_Pedagogy_of_Compassion_at_the_Heart_of_HE (accessed 2 October 2023).

2.2.4 Building 'Coalitions' with Students[22]

Just as I have found it useful to work more with colleagues since taking on a leadership role and as I encourage students to engage with people they perceive as different to them, I have relished opportunities to work collaboratively with a broad range of students within my school and beyond. Student support should be about partnership with students as much as anything else in higher education. I have found the most rewarding moments have come from discussing my positionality with students and creating spaces where we share our identities and backgrounds together. For example, in partnership with students, we set up a Community Hub as an alternative social space for students who identify as under-represented.[23] We talk and learn on mutual ground without me trying to impose or suggest solutions but simply showing my solidarity with these students. This group has gone on to become fully student led and is making a significant contribution to student community building in the school. In this space and others, students see me using my position to amplify and embed under-represented voices and perspectives wherever I can. I also work with students as co-researchers and co-designers, building on students as partners' pedagogies.[24] Engaging with students on level playing fields has been really positive in acknowledging my privilege and humbling to learn how much I don't know because it is not my lived experience. However, this lack of knowledge hasn't made me feel like an 'impostor' as other hidden aspects of the university have. Instead, it empowers me to continue learning, every day, in all aspects of my life. Students know through this approach that they are never just statistics to me and that my work is always done with the aim of making the school and university a better place for them.

I had the privilege recently of chairing a keynote panel delivered by some of the under-represented student co-designers I partnered with to co-design a reverse mentoring project. We opened the Student Education Conference at the University of Leeds and it was genuinely one of my career highlights to

---

[22] Inspired by Emma Dabiri, *What White People Can Do Next: From Allyship to Coalition* (Harper Perennial, 2021).

[23] See essl.leeds.ac.uk/law/news/article/1554/school-of-law-launches-community-hub (accessed 2 October 2023).

[24] Ibid and see Rachael O'Connor and Grave Pountney, 'Celebrating the value of co-creating student-focussed research in partnership with under-represented students' at 145 in Alison Cook-Sather et al, 'The art of partnership: Expanding representations and interpretations' (2022) 6(2) International Journal for Students as Partners 135–52. See also Rachael O'Connor, 'Do you identify as under-represented?' A wellness focused exploration of co-designing a reverse mentoring scheme in partnership with under-represented students' (2023) Journal of Educational Innovation, Partnership and Change (forthcoming).

date. Although not a publication, this authentic dissemination of student voices in the academic arena attempted to challenge some of the criticisms around students as partners work and the lack of opportunity students get to engage in dissemination.[25] Such activist work has to be done *with* students, not just *by* me, challenging the neoliberal rhetoric of students as passive consumers and instead, recognising them as the lifeblood of our roles.[26]

2.3 REMEMBERING THE BIGGER PICTURE: WHAT ARE PEOPLE REALISTICALLY ABLE TO DO?

With hindsight, I have been guilty in the past of overly focussing on student experiences, perhaps to the detriment of colleague workloads. The balance, particularly in the COVID-19 pandemic era, has been hard to strike. I was trained in a profession where every six minutes of my day were recorded and only really mattered if they could be billed to clients.[27] The need to meet and often exceed time and billing targets meant that the concept of manageable workload was fairly alien to me and is something that I am still adjusting to, finding that workload can often be used to stop me pursuing opportunities, which can feel frustrating. That 'corporate lawyer mentality' followed me into academia and I still find myself committing to unworkloaded tasks, even when I know I am at capacity. I have real 'FOMO'[28] when it comes to all things student support/education.

Consequently, I have sometimes judged student support provision based on my own (sometimes incorrect) standards and capacity without acknowledging that as a staff community, we all have different demands and that sometimes my approach may not be sustainable for everyone. There is a risk in student support leadership roles of going too far 'above and beyond' and expecting colleagues to achieve that same standard which may be unrealistic for someone who does not have the workload allocation of a leadership role.[29] Failing to be cognisant of this may create unintentional frictions with colleagues. The more I collaborate with and listen to colleagues, the more I have come to appreci-

---

[25] Lucy Mercer-Mapstone et al, 'A systematic literature review of students as partners in higher education' (2017) 1(1) International Journal for Students as Partners 14–15.
[26] Cf. Shuab Gamote et al, 'Student Partnership to Achieve Cultural Change' (2022) 6(1) International Journal of Students as Partners 99–108.
[27] Cf. Cheryl Krause and Jane Chong, 'Lawyer Wellbeing as a Crisis of the Profession' (2019) 71 South Carolina Law Review 203–44.
[28] 'Fear of missing out'.
[29] See Chapter 4 on knowing where to draw the line when supporting students and Chapter 5 on setting boundaries.

ate this. Here are some practical tips that have helped me to better support colleagues:

2.3.1 Make Lives Easier but Leave Space for Individuality

Recognising mounting workloads in terms of student support and personal tutoring since the COVID-19 pandemic, I try to do things that: (i) improve student support/staff and student contact, and (ii) make colleagues' lives easier and enable them to interpret different student support initiatives in ways that work for them. I have found this particularly useful for personal tutoring. For example, if asking colleagues to run a group tutee session, I provide them with a template that gives ideas of activities/discussion points but leaves space for the tutor to put their own stamp on it, rather than just specifying 'meeting 1 should be about x; meeting 2 should be about y.' This can be a great way to try to ensure there is consistency and a baseline standard in terms of tutoring provision, increasing the chances of key messages getting to students in a way that gives colleagues freedom to bring their authentic selves to sessions. It also encourages colleagues to consider critical issues like sense of belonging in their everyday practice which may not otherwise be on their radar.[30]

2.3.2 Listening to and Respecting the Realities of Others

We can't get everyone on board with the all-singing, all-dancing, jazz hands version of what we might want student support to be. It has been a hard journey for me to come to this realisation. As hard as we try, some people don't believe in certain things in the same way you might. For example, my passion is creating personalised and authentic staff/student relationships and eradicating hierarchies. If a student referred to me as a good friend or their university mum (preferably sister!), that would make me happy – that signifies trust. For other colleagues, this might be something they fundamentally disagree with or can never see themselves achieving. We all have different strengths and perceptions of success. Other colleagues may not have the time/capacity to commit in the same way to student support that we can in our roles. This is where giving regular opportunities for discussion with colleagues (and students) has been important. For example, through student surveys or having whole School discussions about sense of belonging and how we can better facilitate

---

[30] On the theme of student belonging work being everyone's job, see Tom Lowe and Ben Jackson (HEPI, 2022), available at: wonkhe.com/blogs/what-does-it-mean-to-become-a-student-in-higher-education/ (accessed 2 October 2023). See also Chapter 11 for some tips on personal tutoring.

it for everyone in our community so that these issues can be positioned in different contexts and individual experiences, not just my view of how they can be addressed – a people centred approach. Discovering the power of this in my school leadership role has significantly fed into my community centred approach to my university-level role.[31]

2.4　FINDING 'YOUR PEOPLE' IN A RESEARCH-FOCUSSED SECTOR

If you are the only person in a role, it can feel very isolating. Sometimes I find myself asking 'does anybody else even care about *insert student support initiative here*?' Or is research and funding all that matters?'[32] Finding 'my people'[33] in the student support/education sphere has been vital in enhancing my wellbeing and remembering that what I do with others has a hugely positive purpose and comes from a good place, even if it may be met with resistance from others at times. I want to share how I have built my network so far to reach this positive place.

2.4.1　Explore Beyond Your School Gates

I have built a really positive network through institutional and external groups.[34] Engaging with people beyond your institution provides opportunity to learn from others involved in student support in different disciplines which has given me more ideas than I have time to implement or act on! It is also an opportunity to share my work and potentially use it to contribute towards institutional and external initiatives (all good for career development). I've found it can also help colleagues within my school to get on board with student support initiatives if they see that it relates to practices across campus or the sector. I've also found social media a really useful space to find out about groups and initiatives in my institution and beyond, as well as key legal education groups' newsletters.[35]

---

[31] See forstaff.leeds.ac.uk/ news/ article/ 8211/ inside -track -a -community -led -approach-to-academic-personal-tutoring (accessed 19 October 2023).

[32] Cf. Malcolm Tight, 'Examining the research/teaching nexus' (2016) 6(4) European Journal of Higher Education 293–311 and Brewster et al (n 1).

[33] See ch 11 on the importance of this for students too.

[34] See e.g., Leeds Institute for Teaching Excellence, available at: teachingexcellence.leeds.ac.uk/, Connecting Legal Education, available at: lawteacher.ac.uk/ uncategorized/connecting-legal-education/ and Advancing Wellness in Law, available at: advancingwellnessinlaw.wordpress.com/ (all accessed 2 October 2023).

[35] See e.g., lawteacher.ac.uk/ (accessed 2 October 2023).

2.4.2 Put Yourself 'Out There'

I spent the first year of my role constantly thinking of myself as a junior who had little to offer to those I perceive as more experienced than me. All that did was hold me back. I built up confidence by presenting my work at different education focussed conferences and, in 2021, I applied for an internal fellowship to create more time to spend on my staff/student reverse mentoring and personal tutoring work.[36] All the voices in my head said 'you're not ready' and 'why would they give this to you?' but I pushed them aside and went for it. It has been a huge catalyst for my career development to date, giving me continuous opportunities to meet new people, be and display my authentic self, and share my work within higher education and beyond. It has made me incredibly happy in the last year to have been invited to speak at sessions/events, something I never imagined would happen to *me* – that stuff is for other people, I always thought. But I was wrong – there is space for a working-class 'pracademic'[37] to contribute meaningfully to institutional initiatives and international communities. It also led to me being offered my current institutional student support leadership role. My network on campus and outside of it has been a crucially important factor in being able to take the scholarship/research side of my student support role further. It has inspired me to believe in myself more and not get so bogged down with focusing on those who put barriers up in favour of maintaining the status quo.[38]

2.4.3 Be the Catalyst

If you can't find anything in your institution or workplace that speaks to who you are and/or what you care about, why not set up a network? Some of my colleagues started a 'working-class in academia' podcast series. It's been a joy to be part of as I discover others around me have experienced similar faux 'impostor syndrome.' We have since set up an institutional network for staff who identify as working-class and it has had huge interest/support. We recently advised an internal research network about the importance of including working-class voices within their strategy and it has been really fulfilling

---

[36] See teachingexcellence.leeds.ac.uk/exploring-academic-personal-tutoring-in-partnership-with-under-represented-students/ (accessed 2 October 2023). See also timeshighereducation.com/campus/authors/rachael-oconnor (accessed 19 October 2023).

[37] Jill Dickinson, Andrea Fowler and Teri-Lisa Griffiths, 'Pracademics? Exploring transitions and professional identities in higher education' (2022) 47(2) Studies in Higher Education 290.

[38] Cf. Bleasdale (n 3); on disrupting the status quo, see also Chapter 8.

to be able to raise the profile of working-class identities across the university.[39] It has amazed me how cathartic these initiatives have been for me. It took some confidence to put myself 'out there' with students and colleagues as someone who feels under-represented. It felt a bit like 'breaking the fourth wall', yet is such a clear display of me 'practicing what I preach' that it has become a fundamental part of my leadership practice. I have also used some of the tips noted above to find other people research in the same area as me (reverse mentoring) and we have built our own network through our shared commitment to dismantling staff/student barriers.

2.5 NAVIGATING UNHEALTHY HIERARCHIES

Academia is historically a very hierarchical discipline with titles and accolades denoting seniority and thereby a person's perceived worth or value.[40] As I ruminated on above, research can often take precedence over student education work in 'the academy', although this is institution dependent. A further issue is that being in a leadership role as an early career academic can involve having to ask more senior colleagues to do things and potentially raise concerns about the way they do (or don't do) things. I have found myself in a strange position where I have no authority to take disciplinary action (nor would I want to) which means issues are raised by students with me and then the staff side is left with managerial colleagues. Sometimes, there has been no further information on what happened next and I haven't always been sure that changes have been made or actions taken. Such situations have created challenging situations with students as I have not been able to provide them with reassurance that things will improve or any definitive outcome. This takes its toll on my wellbeing as I feel that I have left students in the lurch to either try and rebuild a potentially damaged relationship or lose out on the tutor relationship altogether, something I believe is a critical part of the university experience as one of the only in-depth one-to-one relationships a student may have with an academic.[41] Alternatively, I might end up taking the student on myself as an 'ad hoc' tutee without workload recognition.[42]

---

[39] Inspired by Emma Heron, 'Friendship as method: reflections on a new approach to understanding student experiences in higher education' (2020) 44(3) Journal of Further and Higher Education 393.

[40] Linda Croxford and David Raffe, 'The iron law of hierarchy? Institutional differentiation in UK higher education' (2015) 40(9) Studies in Higher Education 1625–40.

[41] Cf. Kathryn J. McFarlane, 'Tutoring the tutors: Supporting effective personal tutoring' (2016) 17(1) Active Learning in Higher Education 78 on the connection with personal tutoring and sense of belonging.

[42] See Brewster et al (n 1) 6. See also Chapter 6.

You may be unsurprised to hear that I haven't got 'an answer' to this – dismantling the well-entrenched hierarchical structure of higher education will take time.[43] I believe we all have a role to play in it and the work I do and that you do (or will do) in your student leadership role contributes to this.

2.5.1 Don't Give Up

Reflect and regularly remind yourself that what you do is important. Sometimes we have to play 'the game' in academia but that doesn't mean we give up on ambitions of creating meaningful change in student support. In my leadership role, I have had to compromise with ideas and proposals relating to student support and personal tutoring specifically. Despite concerns it wouldn't work, I held onto a proposal I made for a staff/student reverse mentoring scheme: this has been the piece of work that kick-started my career, my fellowship and all of the opportunities I have today. It has given me my 'niche' that at times, I never thought I would have. I have introduced parts of my personal tutoring vision over time and have had input into institutional level developments. I am now conducting a cross-campus project exploring institutional personal tutoring policies in partnership with staff and under-represented students which I am continuing through my university leadership role. What can feel impossible at the start of your leadership journey may become more feasible as you gain more experience and start to better understand 'the system.' We talk about the hidden curriculum for students[44] but there is also a hidden institution for staff who don't fit the 'traditional' mould of an academic. Challenging and dismantling this will take time and collective effort, but we can achieve it by continuing to amplify authentic voices and not allowing perceived levels of seniority or hierarchy to stop us from attempting to bring about change.

2.5.2 Seek Support from Other Leaders

As explained above, at first, I didn't make the most out of opportunities to collaborate with colleagues in other roles, despite their areas such as assessment or diversity and inclusion being closely intertwined with student support. Once I got to grips with how to do this effectively, more collaboration and discussion has helped me to form bonds with colleagues in other student leadership roles. This has given me greater confidence when proposing ideas to management or central leadership when I can draw on others' areas and explain the impact of

---

[43] See Bleasdale (n 3).
[44] Cf. qaa.ac.uk/news-events/news/unpacking-the-hidden-curriculum-for-students-new-guidance-launched-for-staff (accessed 2 October 2023).

proposals. It has contributed to my broader understanding of the rules of the game in the 'field' of higher education and how to play it a little better.[45]

2.5.3 The Power of Conversation

When faced with a rude e-mail in a work context, there is always temptation to 'bite back'. However, that never made me feel better because it was an affront to my authenticity, to who I am – a person who values positive conversations over conflict. My motto for this in legal practice was always 'kill them with kindness:' this applies well to navigating hierarchies of academia too. I have a whiteboard in my office and written on it in big letters for a long time was 'when you know better, do better'[46] and I do know better, so what's my excuse? Instead of battling with colleagues over issues relating to student support, I make time to speak with them so that we can understand each other's perspectives and hopefully come to amicable solutions that work for both students and staff as a community, rather than viewing it as 'us vs them' or 'senior vs junior.' In doing this, I feel in a small way that I am challenging the hierarchies and norms of higher education and this aligns more broadly with the focus of my research.[47]

2.6 THE POWER OF AUTHENTICITY TO SUPPORT CULTURAL CHANGE: YOU ARE NOT AN IMPOSTOR

When I first came to academia, I felt reluctant to reveal the real 'me' and didn't see it as part of my role to do so, just as I had hidden my background when I was in private practice. As well as labels of 'didn't go to Oxbridge', 'didn't go to private school', 'comes from a working-class background' that silently but sometimes menacingly followed me around in the legal profession, becoming more acute in certain social situations, I acquired the label 'doesn't have a PhD' – another thing to add to the 'I don't belong' list.[48] This inevitably bred

---

[45] Cf. Ann-Marie Bathmaker, 'Thinking with Bourdieu: thinking after Bourdieu. Using "field" to consider in/equalities in the changing field of English higher education' (2015) 45(1) Cambridge Journal of Education 61.
[46] Taken from the legendary Maya Angelou.
[47] Rachael O'Connor, 'Supporting students to better support themselves through reverse mentoring: the power of positive staff/student relationships and authentic conversations in the law school' (2023) 57(3) The Law Teacher 253–70. https://www.tandfonline.com/doi/full/10.1080/03069400.2023.2206738 (accessed 14 December 2023).
[48] On this, see Dickinson et al (n 37) 300–301.

feelings associated with 'impostor syndrome.' How many times do you hear or have you personally said 'I suffer from impostor syndrome'? I have heard so many students and colleagues, including myself, use this phrase as a tool to convince themselves they can't succeed or don't belong. My perspective on this changed as I delved into research on impostor phenomenon when I was studying for my post-graduate academic teaching qualification.[49] I realised the problem wasn't me or others around me who also come from different under-represented backgrounds. The problem is the system, the environment, the reproduction of hierarchy and tradition that exists in our sector (and many others). Within that process of unlearning about impostor syndrome and learning about impostor phenomenon, I started to feel more confident to be me and encourage students and colleagues to do the same.

Most notably, in working with students from under-represented backgrounds, I have learned the importance of sharing myself with students and colleagues, leading by example. I have found it can help others understand where I'm coming from when I ask them to do things like 'tell students about a time you perceived yourself as failing and how it made you feel/what steps you took to address those feelings;'[50] or when I'm asking students from working-class backgrounds to take part in activities like listening rooms to share their experiences or to mentor staff and share their lived experiences. A regular reminder that I am human[51] can encourage others to reflect on what makes them human and how they can bring this into their university relationships, which may be in a very different way to me. Just as sharing our positionality can make research more credible,[52] it can make our daily practice more credible too. However, I acknowledge this is easier for me to do because I don't have any particular trauma attached to my background. The ability or desire to do this may be very different for people with similar or different under-represented identities and this must be respected and supported.

If it isn't something you have done before, I encourage you to think about that simple question: who are you? What is important to you? What aspects of

---

[49] Queena Hoang, 'The Impostor Phenomenon: Overcoming Internalized Barriers and Recognizing Achievements' (2013) 34(6) The Vermont Connection 42 and Simpkins (n 7).
[50] On the value of sharing our weaknesses with students, see Chapter 5 and Chapter 9.
[51] Ibid on humanisation. See also Rachael O'Connor, '"It makes me feel empowered and that we can make a difference": Reverse mentoring between international students and staff in legal education' (2022) 3(1) European Journal of Legal Education 95–126.
[52] On researcher positionality, see e.g., Lucy Avraamidou, '"I am a young immigrant woman doing physics and on top of that I am Muslim": Identities, intersections, and negotiations' (2020) 57 Journal of Research in Science Teaching 323–24.

your background and life are critical to your identity and how do/can you bring that into your student support practice? Here are some of the ways I try to do it:

2.6.1 Authentic Introductions and Connections

I started small and grew in confidence with this myself. For example, I started by using an 'about me' slide in small group teaching, progressed to using it in bigger lectures, before then starting keynote conference presentations with it and giving a TedX talk built upon identity,[53] all of which allow me to value the power of being my authentic self in all spaces. That way, people can hopefully see my authenticity from the outset and recognise that the things I do come from an honest place. As well as my hobbies and the Humber bridge as a nod to my working-class roots, my dog always features in this slide. Rudy, this chapter is dedicated to you as my ultimate source of wellness! Finding other people who also share this passion to be authentic with students and colleagues has been critical to building this self-confidence as others support me to see the importance of identity and sharing that with others.

2.6.2 Ask People Who They Are

Be aware, some people may find this disconcerting (particularly new students) but there is positivity and change in getting comfortable in the uncomfortable – be 'the domino.'[54] For example, when I initially meet a student as their personal tutor or dissertation supervisor, I focus that session on getting to know each other. Often, it's met with a bit of surprise as students expect to be immediately grilled on their grades and academic work but if we do this, we tell students that who they are as people has no space in academia, perpetuating the problems that currently exist in the system. Lack of space and time to personalise relationships contributes towards a sense that students need to assimilate. I take advantage of every opportunity to talk to students and colleagues about their identities to embed the view that it is as important as anything else within their degree or career and encourage them to speak out against others who seek to undermine this.

---

[53] See https://www.youtube.com/watch?app=desktop&v=cVRcnwbo3kg (accessed 14 December 2023).
[54] See ted.com/talks/luvvie_ajayi_jones_get_comfortable_with_being _uncomfortable?language=en (accessed 2 October 2023).

2.6.3 Carry Out Authentic Student Support Work

I opened this chapter by inviting you to determine my credibility as an author on this topic by telling you about my positionality. This has also been the driver for my research/scholarship work, and I make this clear whenever I talk about it. This isn't to say that you shouldn't do work with students from backgrounds that are different to your own (this is one of the joys and learning opportunities of such research) but I have found it important to be open and honest about who I am, my privilege and the huge gaps in my knowledge/lived experiences, which have led to me working with students as research partners. Beyond research, I strive to ensure under-represented student voices are included meaningfully in decision making. For example, I hired six students who self-identify as under-represented to co-design and deliver welcome and induction activities in our school. This not only supported the development of a student priority focused welcome and induction but empowered these six students in terms of their own sense of belonging in our community.

2.7 SUMMARY

I hope you've valued this dive into my experiences as an early career academic in a student support leadership role and that you have been able to reflect on your own path and experiences throughout. I'll finish with my top tips for enjoying and succeeding in student support leadership roles as an early career academic whilst prioritising your wellbeing in the process:

1. Remember you are only one person: although you might like to, you don't have all the solutions to what are often institutional and sector-wide issues. You also can't do everything at once. There's always something else. It might be something new, something exciting, something that might get you promoted more than the other thing you've already committed to. But make your choices wisely and strategically if you're aiming towards a future next step (such as promotion), making sure you keep time to be you.
2. Don't put yourself in a box: the way you start out in a role doesn't have to be the way you continue or the way you end. I thought I would never be a 'researcher' given my teaching and scholarship contract. I put myself in a box that said 'not a researcher' because people told me what I do is scholarship. But now I've broken out of that box – I proudly call myself a researcher and know that I am one, regardless of what contract I work on or my title. It's ok to change – embrace it and celebrate the hard work and resilience it takes.

3. Collaborate with people who lift you up: I class the editor of this book as one of 'my people' so this chapter in itself is prime evidence of how surrounding yourself with positive influences who care about the same issues as you can lift you up, e.g. by inviting you to write a chapter in their book. Don't overlook students here – working in partnership with them can be one of the most uplifting and rewarding parts of the journey.
4. Reflect regularly: think about what you have achieved, how it's contributing towards your school/faculty/university goals and towards where you want to be – your next role, promotion, job satisfaction, values etc. Keep a note of all this somewhere so you can use it strategically when you need to and to remind yourself how far you've come and all you've contributed on the tough days.
5. Don't buy into the 'impostor syndrome' hype: be yourself – you deserve to be in your role, you are capable. You don't have a syndrome but you work in a sector whose structures and hierarchies may make you and others feel excluded. We all have a role to play in changing the system for the better so why not be ourselves whilst we do it?

3. Looking back to look forward: scaffolding the student support pathway for students through the eyes of an early career legal academic

Laura Hughes-Gerber, Noel McGuirk, Rafael Savva

3.1 INTRODUCTION

As an early career legal academic, there are many ways in which you will engage with your students throughout the course of their studies. Principally, you will be tasked with facilitating knowledge creation and exchange by developing learning and teaching activities. However, you will likely also be responsible for providing students with some form of academic or pastoral support.[1] Our chapter is concerned with the latter, and its aim is simple: to provide you with an insight into our approach to student support to help you reflect on yours and consider whether (and where) there is room for improvement. At the outset, we would like to highlight that the advice provided in this book is drawn from our own experience in our respective roles as legal academics and from preliminary research undertaken in the field of legal education.

Students by their very nature are diverse, requiring a wide and dynamic range of support streams tasked to assist them with becoming effective independent learners.[2] The COVID-19 pandemic and the ensuing UK government lockdowns from March 2020 onwards, as well as the normalisation of conversations around physical and mental health and social issues affecting

---

[1] There is much literature on defining academic support and pastoral care in the context of legal education. For a general discussion in relation to this, see Kristine S. Knaplund and Richard H. Sander, 'The Art and Science of Academic Support' (1995) 45(2) Journal of Legal Education 157; and Paula Lustbader, 'From Dreams to Reality: The Emerging Role of Law School Academic Support Programs' (1997) 31 University of San Francisco Law Review 839.

[2] See also Chapter 11.

student retention and experience, have accentuated student support needs, which now prove to have a continuing impact on the student learning process. In this chapter, we explore ways of approaching student support in the course of fulfilling your role as a legal academic. The suggestions and tips provided throughout this chapter are not represented as being the only way to proceed. Rather, they offer a structured starting point to addressing student support needs alongside other techniques and approaches you can utilise, some of which can be found in other chapters of this book.

3.2 A PRIMER ON STUDENT SUPPORT

Step into the shoes of your past, undergraduate student self. At some point, you will have accessed or felt like you needed to access some form of support. Such support could have been provided by your peers, professional services staff or ultimately the academic staff teaching you. Maybe you wanted to clarify a point in a module you found confusing or hard to grasp. You might have been anxious about your progression and needed support. Equally, you might have needed support beyond the realm of academic matters. You may for example have had financial difficulties or a health problem precluding you from studying effectively.

Looking back on these experiences, can you still say if the support provided by your department or university, if any, was helpful? If not, to what extent was it unhelpful? Can you also say why you came to this conclusion? By now, you may have arrived at somewhat different conclusions to those of other readers. Differing experiences prior to entering university and variations in cultural attributes often mean students have different interactions with, and perceptions about, accessing student support. The roles developed to provide student support, the accessibility of the support provided and the attentiveness of the staff providing it might also have been conducive to the shaping of your experience.[3]

Combining our reflections on our past experiences with our interactions with students in our roles as legal academics, we arrived at the conclusion that the disparities in students' experiences with student support must be expected and addressed in the course of providing student support. The diverse support needs of students may however lead to confusion amongst students as to *what* kind of support is available, *where* they can access that support and *who* is capable of providing such support. At the same time, students' differing needs are often such that distinguishing them in the foregoing manner is practically difficult to achieve for us as academics, let alone for students themselves.

---

[3] See also Chapter 4.

The turmoil the COVID-19 pandemic brought to academia, alongside the greater awareness gained as to student needs, had us faced with an uncomfortable truth: the structures and systems of student support require re-calibration and stress-testing to cater for students' support needs even in the most difficult of circumstances.[4] Our research in this area suggests not only that student support should be provided holistically, combining the provision of academic support and pastoral care, but that it should also be provided as such across multiple streams of student support.[5]

While we have initial suggestions as to how the holistic provision of student support may be workable in practice,[6] we are still probed with seeking to answer two principal questions. First, how should a system of student support work to provide academic support and pastoral care holistically at a departmental and institutional level? Secondly, how can legal academics provide academic support and pastoral care holistically in their respective roles, whether that be the traditional role of a lecturer or tutor, or a more specific one, such as a role dedicated to providing additional academic support and/or as the main departmental point of contact for pastoral care? This chapter endeavours to shed some light on the second question, which is principally drawn from our experience gained in student support roles at Lancaster University Law School.[7]

3.3 GETTING TO KNOW OUR STUDENTS

The approach we adopt in this chapter is to create a range of fictional personas aimed towards reflecting some of the students you will likely encounter over the course of your career. This approach aligns with service design thinking as the means to simulate student experiences to allow us to map different ways in which students can be supported.[8] As with any chapter, there is a limit to the amount of space we can dedicate to personas but we hope that at least some

---

[4] Cf. Pradeep Sahu, 'Closure of Universities Due to Coronavirus Disease 2019 (COVID-19): Impact on Education and Mental Health of Students and Academic Staff' (2020) 12(4) Cureus e7541.

[5] Cf. (forthcoming) Laura Hughes-Gerber, Noel McGuirk and Rafael Savva, 'Sculpting the Provision of Student Support for Law Students to enhance inclusivity: complications and challenges' (Erasmus Law Review, forthcoming Spring 2024). Also see Noel McGuirk, Rafael Savva and Laura Hughes-Gerber, 'Embedding compassion into law curricula: the role of compassion pedagogy' (2023) 31(1), Nottingham Law Journal, 42-53.

[6] Ibid.

[7] See also Chapter 5.

[8] Michael Doherty and Tina McKee, 'Service design comes to Blackstone's tower: Applying design thinking to curriculum development in legal education' in Emily

of these characters partially reflect your students. Personas have been used in a variety of industries as the means to test ideas and suggest pathways.[9] Through the use of personas, we can emulate real-life student diversity and life-like student support needs to enable us to reflect on how we, as academics, can best support them.

3.3.1 The Role of the Legal Academic

What is the role of a legal academic in supporting students?[10] You will know that there is no easy answer to this question as your role is unique and likely also dynamic.[11] When it comes to providing student support, we have found that there are three factors that have helped us to effectively support our students. First, keeping alert to the different student stress points in the academic year from the anxiety of starting university to the demands of studying Law, keeping on top of deadlines and completing assessments, perhaps also whilst trying to complete paid work and/or work experience. These activities create stress points in the year that pose challenges to our students and if we are alert to them then it becomes easier to proactively identify students who might be struggling. Second, we have found that using the available data on attendance and assessment submissions can be a key indicator of a student support need. Third, the use of formal and informally scheduled meetings throughout the year provides the means to check in on a student's progress and their welfare.

3.3.2 Approach to Student Support

Now that we have established the importance of student support, and its holistic provision, the question then turns to the role of the ECR legal academic

---

Allbon and Amanda Perry-Kessaris (eds), *Design in Legal Education* (Routledge, 2022).

[9] Cf. Mariana Lilley, Andrew Pyper and Susan Attwood, 'Understanding the Student Experience Through the Use of Personas' (2012) 11(1) Innovation in Teaching and Learning in Information and Computer Sciences 4–13; Steve Mulder and Ziv Yaar, *The User is Always Right, A Practical Guide to Creating and Using Personas for the* Web (New Riders, 2007); John Pruitt and Tamara Adlin, *The Persona Lifecycle, Keeping People in Mind Throughout Product Design* (Elsevier Inc, 2006).

[10] For further discussion of the ambiguity in the role of the academic supporting students, see Gareth Hughes, Mehr Panjwani, Priya Tulcidas and Nicola Byron, 'Student Mental Health: The Role and Experiences of Academics' Student Minds (2018), p. 19, available at: studentminds.org.uk/uploads/3/7/8/4/3784584/180129_student_mental_health__the_role_and_experience_of_academics__student_minds_pdf.pdf (accessed 2 October 2023).

[11] See also Chapter 9.

in structuring support to your students in practice. Our approach to student support can be summarised by way of the 'CADSIF' formula.[12] This is not intended to be either restrictive or prescriptive, rather it should be used as a general point of orientation in approaching student support:

1. **Contact – establish contact with the student:** The appropriate way to establish initial contact will depend on the nature of the situation and may be established by the student themself should they approach you directly. It could also be facilitated by a colleague or it could be down to you to approach the student and to determine the best means of doing so. It is important to note that institutional norms may dictate and/or restrict the available/appropriate means of communication, for example some institutions require that all electronic correspondence between staff and students be directed to a university email address.
2. **Assurance – reassure the student that you are here to help them and that they are doing the right thing in speaking to you:** it is important for the student to know that this is a safe space. Whilst you should not provide guarantees as to confidentiality (as depending on what the student divulges, you may be obliged to inform student wellbeing services), you should assure the student that they are taking the important first step in the support pathway and ensure that they are made to feel comfortable speaking to you.
3. **Dialogue – have an open and honest dialogue with the student. What are their concerns? What is the impact upon their studies?:** it is important to listen patiently and sympathetically to the student's concerns. It can be intimidating for students to open up, perhaps for the first time, about something which could be deeply personal to them. It is important to foster an open and honest dialogue with the student to ensure that you are in a position to advise them appropriately.
4. **Signpost to appropriate institutional and external support mechanisms:**[13] As academics we cannot purport to be able to solve all our students' problems, as much as we would like to. What we can do is signpost

---

[12] This approach is inspired by the Mental Health First Aider Action Plan: ALGEE. Cf. MHFA England, 'Being a Mental Health First Aider, Your Guide to the Role' (2021), available at: mentalhealthatwork.org.uk/resource/being-a-mental-health-first-aider-your-guide-to-the-role/ (accessed 2 October 2023).

[13] Cf. Gareth Hughes, Rebecca Upsher, Anna Nobili, Ann Kirkman, Christopher Wilson, Tasmin Bowers-Brown, Juliet Foster, Sally Bradley and Nicola Byrom (2022), 'Education for Mental Health', Online: Advance HE, p. 136 et seq on effective signposting, available at: s3.eu-west-2.amazonaws.com/assets.creode.advancehe-document-manager/documents/advance-he/AdvHE_Education%20for%20mental%20health_online_1644243779.pdf (accessed 2 October 2023).

them to appropriate institutional and external support mechanisms. In this regard, it is particularly important to be well-versed in the former.[14]

5. **Information – provide the student with any additional information on appropriate support mechanisms:** Depending on the nature of the student's support needs and the nature of the institutional/external support service you have referred them to, it is good practice to provide them with further information e.g. how do they access said service? Are you able to provide them with an indication as to their waiting time? Can you/is it appropriate to expedite the process via a direct referral from you?

6. **Follow-up to check how the student is progressing and encourage support:** It is important that a student doesn't feel as though departmental support ends with a referral. For this reason, it is good practice to follow-up with a student after meeting with them to establish how they are progressing and to encourage them to continue to engage with appropriate support.

It is common that your student will view you as the academic as having all the answers that will resolve their challenges. However, the reality is that we often have to position ourselves as a listener able to talk the student through their challenges so that they can be signposted to appropriate assistance.

Positioning yourself as a listener whilst remaining alert to key stress points and stress factors throughout the academic year has in our experience proved conducive to helping students feel supported within the department itself. For example, some of the common problems we have found arising in the first term are often related to feelings of loneliness and isolation from students. The difficulty for some first years in this respect is acute. Read on to meet Samir to put this issue into context and to explore how you as an academic can support Samir using the support formula as your starting point.

3.4 SAMIR

3.4.1 Background

Samir is an 18-year-old First Year LLB Law student. Prior to commencing his studies this academic year, Samir achieved AAB in his A Levels. Samir was diagnosed with dyslexia whilst still at school, where he benefited from specialised educational support. He is keen to replicate this at university. Samir was the first in his close-knit family to go to university and initially

---

[14] Hughes, Panjwani, Tulcidas and Byron (n 10) 34.

> felt a little apprehensive about what to expect. Samir lives on campus but travels home on occasional weekends. Alongside his studies, Samir works in retail to supplement his income from his student loan. He tends to work in varying shift patterns totalling between 15-20 hours per week. Samir has a close circle of friends and family. He is already an enthusiastic member of the university Law Society, as well as a keen footballer. Samir is interested in a career at an international Law firm, though he also remains open-minded in respect of other career paths.

3.4.2 Student's Experience

After Samir moves to university, he finds the welcome week activities a little intimidating with so many people around and as he generally finds it difficult to start conversations, he doesn't manage to make any friends. Samir finds his flatmates difficult to get on with as they don't share his interests. During Samir's first week, he meets with his academic advisor who is very focused on providing advice on his studies. Although Samir hopes that once his classes begin he will soon settle into his studies, in the first few weeks of term, Samir's challenges worsen. He finds the sheer number of students in lecture halls to be overwhelming. In the smaller group sessions, Samir finds that as he doesn't know anyone, he is terrified of answering questions in case he gets the answer wrong. As the first month progresses, Samir also feels he can't go to lectures as he can't keep track of the topics with so many fellow students attending.

3.4.3 Supporting Samir

Samir's attendance dips and after an attendance check, you write to Samir as his academic advisor to set up a meeting to understand why he has stopped attending his classes (**Contact**). Now that Samir is coming to see you, how would you approach this? Reading this, you may think the best approach is a disciplinary approach, reprimanding Samir for failing to attend his classes. In this type of case, we would however advocate that the stronger approach is to assure the student that they are doing the right thing by confiding in you (**Assurance**) and to begin an honest conversation by listening to them (**Dialogue**). The ultimate objective of meeting with Samir is to empower him to find a way to gain the confidence to make friends and take his place in his academic community.

A good way to start the meeting might be to highlight that you are concerned that Samir has just started university and has low attendance which will make the topics harder to study and the assessments harder to pass, with the more content he misses. Part of the problem here is that Samir does not feel part of the academic community. We, as academics, can't help him make friends but we can empower him with support to gain the confidence he needs to begin attending classes. The range of options here might include signposting Samir to a wellbeing session or a professional counselling session/activity to allow him to gain the benefit of professional advice on how to deal with the transition from school to university. There may also be opportunities for students to be referred to a student/peer mentor for help and advice on settling into university or to social groups aligned with his interests (**Signposting**). From the academic perspective, the key expectation is to focus on giving the student some options to empower them to find a solution that will work for them (**Information**). It is also good practice to check back in with the student shortly after the meeting to see what steps Samir has taken to resolve his attendance issue (**Follow-Up**).

3.4.4 Reflection

Of course, not all student support needs arise or are triggered by key stress points in the academic year like Samir's. Other students' support needs may either predate or extend far beyond their studies. Some students' support needs may arise from the curriculum itself.[15] In this regard, further common examples of student challenges at university are the study of Law itself and the challenges that life can throw at us. The loss of a loved and cherished family member, friend or pet, the estrangement of students from their family, the experience of being a victim of a serious assault, a health condition, a relationship breakdown, a caring responsibility or financial challenges all depict personal challenges students may face during the course of their studies. It can be difficult for us, as academics, to support our students in specific ways to manage these challenges. Read on to meet Christine, who puts several of these challenges into context.

3.5 CHRISTINE

3.5.1 Background

Christine is a 46-year-old second-year mature Law student. Prior to commencing her studies, Christine worked in a variety of administration roles in human resources and has long desired a career change. After her divorce a few years ago, Christine decided to return to college and seize upon an op-

---

[15] See also Chapter 10.

> portunity of further study to change her life. Christine has two kids, 10 and 11, with her youngest being on the autism spectrum. This leaves a busy lifestyle for Christine but she really enjoys the challenging pace of her personal life and her studies. Christine has long held the desire to practise as a solicitor and is especially interested in employment or family law. Christine has an active range of hobbies that she likes to pursue in her free time, such as volunteering and baking.

3.5.2 Student's Experience

Christine already has a hectic life with her own family with their own additional needs. After starting second year, Christine is finding the workload extremely difficult to balance with her family life. Her youngest's additional needs consume a lot of Christine's time. The move to online teaching during the pandemic helped Christine to manage her parental responsibilities as she didn't have to leave home, meaning she was able to study and be there for her children. The transition back to in-person teaching is proving difficult: there are lots of classes to go to, the module content is more difficult and there seems to be a perpetual cycle of deadlines. This has resulted in Christine having an impossible balancing exercise between university work and family life. Christine now feels that she is neglecting her children and has begun to feel low in mood. The stress of assessment after assessment, coupled with the needs of her family, has meant that she begins to feel depressed that she can't give her children the time they need.

3.5.3 Supporting Christine

Christine comes to see you as her academic advisor (**Contact**) – so how do you approach this? We are not counsellors or at least not professionally trained counsellors.[16] Nevertheless in supporting students, we should inter alia strive to be empathetic, inclusive, student-centred and committed.[17]

---

[16] Cf. Hughes, Upsher, Nobili, Kirkman, Wilson, Bowers-Brown, Foster, Bradley and Byrom (n 13) 132f.
[17] Cf. UKAT 'UKAT Core Values of Personal Tutoring and Academic Advising', available at: ukat.ac.uk/standards/core-values-of-personal-tutoring-and-academic-advising/ (accessed 2 October 2023). For a resource on supporting student parents specifically, see Andrea Todd 'The Personal Tutor's Guide to Supporting Student-Parents in Higher Education' (UKAT), available at: https://www.ukat.ac.uk/media/yfnnsfjq/the-personal-tutor-guide-to-supporting-student-parents-a-todd.pdf (accessed 27th November 2023).

There is no one perfect solution, in this type of circumstance we have found it common for the student to arrive at your office in the hope that you are going to present them with a solution. The first steps usually involve reassuring the student that they are doing the right thing by speaking to you (**Assurance**) and listening to them (**Dialogue**). This is usually followed by signposting the student for example to university wellbeing services to help Christine to talk through her challenges to help her find a coping mechanism. It is also good practice to refer students with a health issue to their General Practitioner for a medical diagnosis and treatment (**Signposting**).

From a departmental perspective, you are also able to help Christine to mitigate the impact of her health condition and family circumstances upon her studies. For example, you can make her aware of the relevant institutional and departmental processes, such as your institution's exceptional circumstances process and the opportunity to apply for coursework extensions, which are specifically designed to mitigate the impact of student circumstances upon their studies (**Information**). Christine might need reassurance that these processes and policies are designed with these sorts of circumstances in mind: it isn't uncommon for students to feel their situation doesn't warrant such support, frequently comparing themselves to others who they perceive as having a much worse time.

In the short-term, coursework extensions may be able to help Christine to approach her assessments[18] in a systematic and manageable way in light of her difficult circumstances. The exceptional circumstances process may also provide Christine with valuable security should she prove unable to complete an assessment or if her performance in said assessment is impaired by her circumstances. In the medium term and particularly in light of the likely ongoing nature of Christine's circumstances, it is crucial that Christine engages with relevant support to ensure that she is in a position to engage with her studies going forward.[19] This is where you can help Christine by regularly checking in with her to see how she is getting on and to check she is continually supported and in a position to engage with her studies (**Follow-Up**). Sometimes for various reasons, students are reluctant to engage with support.[20] Sometimes they become disillusioned with it when they feel that it isn't helping them quite as much or as quickly as they would wish. In this situation, it may be up to you to persuade Christine to (continue to) engage with support or to reassure her

---

[18] On assessment as conducive to both learning and wellbeing, Hughes, Upsher, Nobili, Kirkman, Wilson, Bowers-Brown, Foster, Bradley and Byrom (n 13) 83f.

[19] Ibid p. 16 on providing support to students who have encountered problems undermining learning and wellbeing as a key principle of curriculum supporting wellbeing and learning.

[20] Hughes, Panjwani, Tulcidas and Byron (n 10) 32.

that her perseverance will pay off. This is crucial not only from an evidentiary perspective as university support processes require evidence but also (and arguably much more importantly) from a wellbeing perspective.

Of course, should Christine's circumstances ever prove to be entirely prohibitive as to engagement with her studies, you can also guide her through the relevant university processes, including the option to pause her academic studies via a period of intercalation. For some students, this option provides them with the time they need to focus on getting themselves back on track and in a position to resume their academic studies.

3.6 WINNIE

3.6.1 Background

> Winnie is a 21-year-old Final Year LLB Law international student. Prior to commencing her studies, Winnie achieved the equivalent of AAA at A Level, in addition to obtaining a merit-based scholarship which has assisted her to attend university abroad. Winnie is the youngest in her family, with both her parents and her older sibling being established professionals. Winnie feels under immense pressure as to both her own and her parents' expectations of her. Winnie is introverted. She would like to be more active socially and in student societies but feels guilty when she is not working towards completing her degree. In line with her parents' expectations, Winnie would like to pursue a career at the bar.

3.6.2 Student's Experience

As a final year, international student, Winnie is facing unique challenges. The former means that Winnie is likely to feel under increased pressure compared to her previous two years of study. She may also be more focused on post-degree career planning than she has been in previous years and preparing pupillage applications and attending interviews may prove difficult to balance with her heavy final-year workload. Winnie's status as an international student also means that she may face unique challenges compared to home students, for example financial pressure stemming from a higher tuition fee burden, a lack of awareness of available NHS services, loneliness and isolation.[21]

---

[21] Cf. e.g., Sidonie Ecochard and Julia Fotheringham, 'International Students' Unique Challenges – Why Understanding International Transitions to Higher Education

3.6.3 Supporting Winnie

Following a seminar, you approach Winnie (**Contact**) as you notice that she has been uncharacteristically quiet in this week's seminar, having not volunteered an answer and having avoided eye contact with you. You listen to Winnie's concerns and reassure her that she is doing the right thing by confiding in you (**Assurance**). Winnie breaks down and admits that she has not been able to prepare for today's seminar. She tells you that she has stayed up all night for the past seven days completing pupillage applications following a rejection from a Chambers she had set her heart on. Winnie says that she is terrified as to how her parents will react should she fail to secure pupillage and obtain a first-class degree. She is unsure how to cope with the pressure and feels completely burnt out (**Dialogue**).

Many of us will find it easy to empathise with Winnie's situation, having felt overwhelmed by the pressure of our own – and others' – expectations of us. In this regard, Winnie would benefit from being referred to both her GP and to student wellbeing services (**Signpost**). As an international student, Winnie may be less familiar with accessing NHS services than a home student would be and may therefore require additional guidance in this respect (**Information**).

You follow up with Winnie two weeks later to see how she is getting along (**Follow-Up**). When you broach the idea of whether she has accessed student wellbeing services, she admits that she has not, explaining that in her own cultural context it is taboo to talk about one's mental health. How can we as academics approach this situation? We do not possess in-depth knowledge of the cultural context of all our students and the impact said context may have on both a student's support needs and their engagement with appropriate support mechanisms. What we can and arguably should do is promote the value of university support services and processes. We can also clarify any misconceptions a student has about accessing support services e.g. that this information could be disclosed to a future employer in a reference or that their parents may find out that they have done so. Both promoting the value of university support services and clarifying misconceptions ultimately helps to tackle and break down the stigma which for some students surrounds their decision as to whether to access university wellbeing services.[22]

Matters' (2017) 5(2) Journal of Perspectives in Applied Academic Practice 100–108. Also see Emmanuel E. Akanwa, 'International Students in Western Developed Countries: History, Challenges, and Prospects' (2015) 5(3) Journal of International Students 271–84.

[22] Hughes, Panjwani, Tulcidas and Byron (n 10) 32.

3.7 PHILIP

3.7.1 Background

> Philip is a 22-year-old undergraduate BA Law and Criminology student. Philip is in the second year of his studies. Prior to commencing his studies, Philip achieved a higher distinction in his BTEC Diploma. Philip had previously attempted a Business and Marketing degree at another university but due to high levels of anxiety, he dropped out at the end of the first year. Philip's anxiety was so bad, he just couldn't complete his written assessments. Philip's mind would go blank and he would feel his heart racing. He was so embarrassed he just withdrew from his studies without engaging with his department. Philip took a break for two years and decided to return to study for a Law and Criminology degree as he wants to become a police officer. He was apprehensive about returning to university as he was a little older than his peers and he was fearful of his anxiety returning. Philip progressed well through first year and passed his assessments first time around. Philip was lucky as he only had one written exam in which he achieved a marginal pass. He lives on campus and has a close relationship with his mother. Philip regularly returns home at the weekend and works locally on campus to supplement his student loan.

3.7.2 Student's Experience

Philip is at the end of the second year of his BA degree and is facing four written exams. Given his experience of written assessments, and the fact he has never reached second year before, he is facing a significant challenge. Will his anxiety resurface, what can he do to manage it and how will his department support him? Philip will likely feel under pressure to complete his assessments so that he can progress to his final year and then onto his dream job.

3.7.3 Supporting Philip

You run an exam workshop to help students prepare for their written assessment in your module. Following the workshop, Philip approaches you **(Contact)** and appears to be quite stressed. He is seeking guidance on the question areas for your written assessment. You are aware from his demeanour that this is more than an attempt to seek out topic areas to help focus his revision. You respond to Philip by reassuring him that he has been to most of your lectures and all the seminars which puts him in pole position for his exams. **(Assurance)**. You also offer him a one-to-one meeting in your office hours so that you can open a dialogue with Philip to explore any potential issues he is facing **(Dialogue)**. During this meeting, you discover Philip's experience of written assessments. Philip confides in you that his anxiety is worse than ever and he is thinking of withdrawing from his studies.

Many of us will find it easy to empathise with Philip as few enjoy completing written assessments but the issue of serious anxiety effectively debilitating a student striving to complete his course will require sensitive ongoing support. The first step here is to signpost Philip to wellbeing and disability services, as well as outside support services such as the GP, to ensure that he obtains the help he needs with his anxiety **(Signpost)**. Signposting to departmental support services such as writing clinics or exam support clinics may also be helpful to support Philip. However, it is also important to think more broadly about how Philip might be supported through these difficult circumstances. It is clear from his experience of assessments that he is at real risk of dropping out of his course. This may prompt a need for you to open a conversation about other options he might have to allow him the space to focus on his health. As his tutor, your primary focus is his health to ensure his wellbeing. In this case, it might involve the difficult decision for Philip to intercalate or pause his studies to give him space away from the assessments to allow him to focus on his wellbeing but also to enable him to return when he is able to complete his studies.

The key information to convey to Philip relates not only to his wellbeing support options but also to his study options so that you can provide him with all the information to help him make an informed decision **(Information)**. This is always a difficult choice for the student and your involvement may be needed in the form of continuous follow-ups with the student. You might provide the student with information to enable them to think about their options so that they can come back and ask further questions to help them decide on their next steps **(Follow-Up)**.

3.8 DO IT YOURSELF

Having considered the support needs of the four personas above, it's now over to you.

> Meet Lewis, who is a 25-year-old postgraduate LLM Law student. Prior to commencing his studies, Lewis acquired a BTEC Level 3 extended diploma and an undergraduate degree from another institution. Lewis found the transition to tertiary level education a challenge, though he benefited from the support offered by his undergraduate institution. Lewis is estranged from

his parents, though he has a close relationship with his younger sister. Lewis lives in private rented accommodation with his long-term partner. He works alongside his studies to supplement his student loan, undertaking frequent bar work on evenings and weekends. Lewis is a conscientious student and is involved in local political campaigning in his free time. Lewis is motivated to use his LLM degree to help others and is thus interested in working in the voluntary sector.

Now imagine yourself in the following situation: A fellow student approaches you for advice in relation to Lewis. His long-term relationship has just broken down, leaving him emotionally distressed but also without a place to live. Lewis cannot go back to his parents' house and, as he is new to the area, he doesn't know how to approach finding accommodation. How would you go about supporting Lewis? Remember **CADSIF**!

Lewis returns to see you later on in the academic year to thank you for your support. You notice that Lewis has become quiet and withdrawn. He confides in you that he is struggling with the isolation of writing his dissertation and is beginning to feel increasingly distanced from his peers. How would you go about supporting Lewis? Remember **CADSIF**!

3.9 KEY POINTS IN SUMMARY

In summary, student support needs are variable and complex in nature and departmental support provision should respond accordingly by treating support needs in an intrinsically holistic manner. Over the course of this chapter, we have reflected upon the role of the legal academic in supporting students by scaffolding the student support pathway for students using the CADSIF formula. We have applied the formula to four separate Law student personas and have invited you to apply it to a fifth Law student persona. In doing so, we hope to have equipped you with a systematic approach to utilise in supporting your students. As educators, we strive to enrich our students educationally but by providing students with appropriate departmental wellbeing support, we can not only facilitate our students achieving their educational goals but vitally we can also ensure that they are sufficiently supported so as to enable them to achieve their potential.

3.10 SUMMARY

1. Student support needs are variable and complex.
2. Student support provision should be holistic.
3. A systematic approach to student support may prove beneficial as a point of reference and orientation.

4. Pastoral support: student views
Georgina May Collins

4.1 INTRODUCTION

We all likely have an opinion on what we think effective pastoral support looks like. Whilst it is important to reflect on our own experiences as learners and educators to inform these views and subsequently our practice, we also need to know what students actually think.[1] This chapter provides an insight into some of the perspectives held by students. The views presented in this chapter were gathered through a series of online focus groups with a range of undergraduate and postgraduate students from law schools across the UK.[2] All UK Universities engaged in teaching Law were invited to participate. Participants were self-selecting and the study involved 20 participants across four groups from a range of institutions. These included small law schools (yearly intake below 100), to large (yearly intake 500+) and included both Russell Group[3] and non-Russell Group universities. The study included a diverse range of students from both undergraduate and postgraduate courses, home/EU and international students. The focus groups were semi-structured, in order to focus on key themes whilst allowing participants to otherwise steer the discussion. Participants have been anonymised and any reference to specific individuals/institutions have been removed. The views expressed in this piece are not intended to represent 'the' student voice but rather reflect a collection of student voices through which we can explore perspectives on pastoral support, and how we can learn and adapt our practice from this.[4]

---

[1] On reflective practice see e.g., Karen Hinett and Tracey Varnava, *Developing Reflective Practice in Legal Education* (UK Centre for Legal Education, 2002).
[2] REC Reference FASSLUMS-2022-0688-RECR-2, Lancaster University.
[3] See russellgroup.ac.uk/ (accessed 2 October 2023).
[4] See also Chapter 2.

4.2 WHAT DO WE MEAN BY 'PASTORAL'?

4.2.1 'I Can't Put My Finger On It. I Can't Say Exactly What It Is'

The term 'pastoral' is frequently used but, as a concept underpinned by 'care,' a universal definition would fail to adequately capture the diverse understandings and experiences of pastoral support.[5] The activities and support captured under the umbrella of 'pastoral' differ between both institutions and individuals.[6] The student perspectives captured during the focus groups reflected these variations, ranging from the pastoral scenes of rolling fields crafted by the romantic poets, to the spiritual guidance of religious institutions. When narrowed to the institutional setting, a number of participants saw pastoral as involving 'support' in a broad sense:

> Support for students to help them stick around and not drop out – you know, to increase their attainment.

Despite this, there were concerns that in practice pastoral support is 'narrow in scope.' In the following section I explore what participants considered to form part of this wide-ranging support before considering how this might influence our practice.

4.2.2 'It's Like Personal'

One theme that emerged was that pastoral support is 'personal.' Personal here had several different meanings. First is that it encompasses personal experiences and barriers; second that the support offered needs to be reflective of the diversity of student experience; and finally that our approach as academics needs to be underpinned by care. Participants emphasised its connection with academic support, and the importance of community and relationship building in providing effective pastoral support.[7]

> Personal might mean anything from academic support to maybe advice or financial support or if you needed to go over like home life or relationships. It was any kind of personal support between you and your tutor.

---

[5] Cf. Nelson E. Soto, 'Caring and relationships: Developing a pedagogy of caring' (2005) 50(4) Villanova Law Review 859, 861.

[6] Cf. Stuart McChlery and Jacqueline Wilkie, 'Pastoral support to undergraduates in higher education' (2009) International Journal of Management Education 23–36.

[7] Cf. Wendy Larcombe et al, 'Does an Improved Experience of Law School Protect Students against Depression, Anxiety and Stress? An Empirical Study of

> Even just coming out and seeing somebody and having a chat with a lecturer about something, or just checking in on you ... like the day-to-day, how're you getting on today?

This need for community and relationship building also requires us to listen to students, to give them space to talk:

> Just listening ... you really are more than enough.

Ensuring students are able to build relationships with their peers and with academics in their department, and creating space for students to speak, underpins effective pastoral support from a student perspective.

This personal approach should also be informed by students' lived experience and their perspectives. In order to provide effective pastoral support, we need to understand the barriers faced by our students, the impact they have on that individual, and respond accordingly:

> We talk about pastoral help then we don't give students space to talk about the kind of real-life issues that affect their learning, and all of the barriers to learning ... if you're aware of what your students are going through you can then support them better.

The need to provide students with the 'space to speak', to feel listened to, and have a sense of belonging is not 'purely' pastoral but clearly has a significant role to play in the learning environment.[8] We should not only acknowledge the diverse perspectives and experiences found in the literature, but also of those studying it. An example given in one of the sessions was land law. Students who do not see homeownership as a prospect, or whose parents don't own property, not only have to manage the intellectual challenge of the topic but the emotional burden too. Acknowledging the diverse ways in which content might impact students, or how they might be perceived from different perspectives, can promote a more inclusive and supportive environment, and signal you care about your students and their experiences.

Wellbeing and the Law School Experience of LLB and JD Students' (2013) 35 Sydney Law Review 407, 425; McChlery and Wilkie (n 6) 23–36.

[8] See also Chapters 2 and 9.

4.2.3 Belonging and Community

Receiving pastoral support was considered essential in helping students to build relationships and a sense of community. Importantly however, having a sense of belonging can itself reduce the need for pastoral support.[9]

> I have been, you know supported from the beginning ... because I did feel isolated at some points.

However, there was an awareness law schools are:

> mostly designed for able bodied, able minded, mostly young, mostly wealthy [people]. Pastoral help should take all of these things into account and...there should be better support.

This speaks to the need for pastoral support to be wide ranging, and reflect students' needs and experiences. We might not always be in the position to address these barriers directly, but there is value in being aware of them, and being open to discussing them with students. Doing so provides a space where students can discuss how factors that might go beyond their academic studies impact them, and allow ourselves as academics to consider whether there is anything we can do. It can make students feel more confident attending or contributing to sessions when the tutor is aware they missed the last session, or haven't quite caught up on the reading, not because they are lazy or not dedicated to their studies, but because of those barriers.

Timetabling, the inability to engage in extra-curricular activities, missing classes, and barriers to relationship building were all raised as factors that should be considered pastoral:

> I don't get involved in extracurriculars. Because ... Who's gonna pick my kid up?

This links back to the need to adopt a 'personal' approach and the importance of community and relationship building. In order to provide appropriate support, we need to understand why students are struggling or not attending:

> going to work to earn money to support my children or going to my lecture. So I would choose to go to work.

---

[9] On the link between community/belonging and student mental health and wellness see e.g., Michael Fay and Yvonne Skipper, 'I was able to ask for help when I became stressed rather than sitting alone and struggling': psychology and law students' views of the impact of identity and community on mental wellbeing (2022) 56(1) The Law Teacher 20–36.

If you notice a student is not attending, gently asking whether there is anything in particular we can do to support their engagement opens up these conversations, and shows we care.

The barriers students face, and the pastoral support they might need so they can engage in their studies are wide-ranging and can be difficult for students to disclose. For example, one participant reflected on their concerns about being 'judged' for being trans which in turn impacted on their attendance and academic performance. They did however note that 'talking to staff helped.' This again emphasises the need for us to build relationships with our students so they feel able to have these conversations, and so we can work with them to provide the support they need.

The lack of flexibility and adaptability in the university system, and the lack of support often faced by students, can then create difficulties in the classroom. Having to attend different sessions where you don't know the other students, or the tutor, can negatively impact a student's wellness and their willingness to actively participate:

> I felt a little reluctant to participate ... everyone is looking at you and you feel a little bit insecure and unsure. Should I talk? I didn't feel comfortable in other groups where I didn't know anyone.

Ensuring pastoral support is integrated into the classroom, creating a welcoming environment, can further supplement the pastoral support offered outside the teaching environment and ensure students are able to engage regardless of their individual circumstances.[10] Checking in with students about barriers to engagement can help us understand why they might not be able to participate despite wishing to do so. For example, timetabling might be beyond our control but if we speak to those students who struggle to attend it might be that we can identify alternative sessions for them to attend, or can offer 1-2-1 support.

4.2.4 Named Roles and Support Services

A number of participants associated pastoral support with those who hold a formalised pastoral role, including central support services such as counselling/mental health or wellbeing.[11] Being clear about what support we can offer in which role we hold, being present, and inviting students to see us rather than

---

[10] See also Chapters 9 and 10.
[11] Randstad, 'A degree of uncertainty: student wellbeing in higher education', available at: randstad .co .uk/ employers/ areas -of -expertise/ student -support/ student -mental-health-report-2020/ (accessed 2 October 2023).

waiting for them to approach us ensures students understand what support we can offer and encourages engagement.[12]

> I've probably seen somebody have the title, pastoral leader at Uni, but they've never spoken to me, they've never emailed me ... I know there is a mental health service, but ... I've never had a pastoral person come into a lecture and say I am this person, this is how I can help.
>
> She just said I'm a personal tutor ... So we've only spoken about academic issues

Having support structures in place does not ensure students are aware of those structures and how to access them. When we actively and consistently make reference to pastoral support we increase the awareness of, and reduce the stigma surrounding, many of the factors potentially leading students to need such support. This also provides us with an opportunity to signpost students towards alternative sources of support. However, signposting should not always be reactive but rather pro-active. Sometimes we can predict when students may need additional support, for example in advance of assessment periods. But we won't always know when each individual student will need a particular type of support. In making pastoral support a part of everyday conversation, by raising it in teaching sessions, by making our roles clear we are able to provide students with the information they need at the time they need it.

Knowing the limits of the support we can and should offer is important as it ensures we can do what is best for the students, and for ourselves.[13] It can be very difficult to know where to draw this 'line' and seeking support and advice from colleagues is invaluable. As an ECR, finding out what is expected of you in relation to pastoral support and familiarising yourself with the support offered by those in formal pastoral roles and central services early on in your post is hugely beneficial.

We should also consider the language we use when referring students to central services. In particular, given the stigma associated with mental ill health there is evidence to suggest that students may be reluctant to seek support from 'Mental Health' services due to the way it has been 'labelled'.[14] So, whilst we may not have the ability to change how these services are 'branded' we can be reassuring in how we speak about them to the students requiring support.

---

[12] See also Chapter 5.
[13] See also Chapters 2, 5 and 6.
[14] Cf. Charles T.R. Walker, 'Wellbeing in higher education: a student perspective' (2022) 40(3) Pastoral Care in Education 310, 315. There is also evidence to indicate that there is similar stigma with 'Disability' e.g., Sue Eccles et al, 'Risk and stigma: students' perceptions and disclosure of "disability" in higher education' (2018) 20(4) Widening Participation and Lifelong Learning 191–208.

4.2.5 So What Does 'Pastoral' Mean?

Although students' views on the meaning of pastoral were wide-ranging there were a number of key themes that emerged. First was that pastoral support is, or should be, personal in nature and in turn needs a personalised approach informed by the individual needs of students. Second was that the ability for students' experiences to feed into both support systems and the curriculum were essential in promoting student wellness and a sense of community and belonging. The relationship building that underpins this in turn has the capacity to increase students' willingness to engage with pastoral support, but may in some cases also lessen the need to do so. Finally, there is a need for staff to be proactive in the support they offer students, and to be clear about their roles and the wider support systems available. This understanding of pastoral care is also echoed in what participants considered to make pastoral support effective.

4.3 EFFECTIVE PASTORAL SUPPORT

This section provides an overview of participants' perspectives on what makes pastoral support effective and allows us to consider how we might adapt our approach to pastoral support to best support student needs.

4.3.1 A Personalised Approach

The importance of having a personalised approach to pastoral support once again emerged from the discussion. Central to this was ensuring we can be responsive to individual needs and view student concerns in context:

> It's about the person-centred support. You need to identify what this individual needs, because not everybody is the same things and we are all different...

Because pastoral care doesn't have a 'one size fits all solution' we need to be able to understand students' diverse needs and experiences, and how we might adapt the advice or support we offer based on this. We cannot model care based on generalised notions of what students need. Even those who share some experiences/characteristics or face similar barriers still might require very different support.[15]

Even the small act of asking whether a student is ok, or whether they'd like to talk to you can be hugely meaningful.[16] There are of course things we, as

---

[15] See also Chapter 11.
[16] On the importance of 'care' in academia see e.g., Steven Meyers, 'Do your students care whether you care about them?' (2009) 57(4) College Teaching 205, 206.

a matter of course, do need to include in response to emails that raise particular concerns, or that we might include in response to an in-person disclosure.[17] However, ensuring we adopt an approach that demonstrates we genuinely care has a profound impact:

> They'll just send you an e-mail back sometimes and they'll be like 'oh you can just find it here, here's the link for you'. They won't even really like genuinely ask if you're ok.

Rather than providing a generic response, adding a personal touch can help students feel seen, listened to, which in turn creates assists in building a positive staff-student relationship where students feel more comfortable opening up:

> You could open up more then and you know get to the bottom of the problem. It feels like someone's actually listening, which is good.

Further to this, relationship building helps us to get to know our students and in turn to 'check when things are off' and identify when a student may need support.[18] It also makes it more likely that students needing support will reach out to us in the first place. This is an element of relationship building that students not only acknowledge, but value:

> It's about what you can both bring to the pastoral relationship. So the more you can engage with it, the more they can get to know you ... they can notice when things are wrong.

As Cahill notes 'for academic and pastoral support to be effective there is a need for student interaction and engagement in the process, a willingness on the behalf of the student to seek advice.'[19] One of the key ways we can ensure this happens is through building reciprocal relationships based on trust, where a student is comfortable approaching you with their concerns, and where you are able to identify when they might be struggling.

---

[17] See also Chapter 9.
[18] On noticing, see John Mason, *Researching Your Own Practice: The Discipline of Noticing* (Routledge, 2002); and Chapter 9.
[19] Jo Cahill et al, 'An Exploration of Undergraduate Student's Views on the Effectiveness of Academic and Pastoral Support' (2014) 56(4) Educational Research 398, 399.

Participants also emphasised the need for understanding and indicated the importance of those providing pastoral support having had similar experiences:

> It helps ... if the person you're talking to has some sort of lived experience of the issue that you're experiencing yourself.

Although they were aware this is something 'you can't always have,' it does emphasise that, where we have had these experiences or faced similar barriers, and if we feel comfortable sharing, it can be a really useful tool in terms of relationship building and the provision of pastoral support.[20] This can be as minimal as sharing that you struggled with a particular subject whilst you were studying, or that you are still completely filled with nerves before giving a lecture. Alternatively, it might involve a more personal disclosure. For example, I frequently share that I was a 'first in family' student from a working-class background. When we share our own experiences and the barriers we have faced it can reassure students you do understand, and helps to establish a reciprocal trusting relationship.

Despite the importance of relationship building and how valuable it can be to share our own experiences this does need to be done whilst ensuring students receive the help they need when approaching us. For example, one of the participants was an international student who had a personal tutor from the same country as them and despite originally being excited about this prospect when meeting with them:

> instead of talking about my mental wellbeing or my work, we started talking about the country and the whole of what is happening back home and stuff like that. And it kind of took the time away and I didn't wanna be rude and interrupt and just say like, please don't speak about this. I'm here for a different reason. So that kind of wasted my time ... and it didn't get me what I wanted either.

The key here is balance. Though sharing our experience and making a connection with our students can be hugely beneficial, we need to ensure that when students approach us they have the opportunity to raise any concerns they might have. It can be really useful to ask students 'if they feel comfortable doing so' to let you know in advance of a meeting why they would like to meet to ensure you're as prepared as you can be to provide the support or signposting that they might need and to make sure you have spoken about that particular issue. In more impromptu situations, or where they have not disclosed in

---

[20] 'A perceived lack of understanding' by lecturers is one of the key factors identified as having a negative impact on student mental health and wellness in Law School by Larcombe et al (n 7) 407, 429. See also Chapters 2, 5, 6 and 8.

advance, checking whether they've had the chance to discuss everything they needed to can also ensure we strike an appropriate balance.

4.4 THE ROLE OF ACADEMICS

The responsibilities of academics in relation to pastoral support, similarly to student mental health, remain 'ambiguous and lacking in clarity. This leads to weak and uncertain boundaries and increased risk to students, staff and universities.'[21] The following provides an overview of participants' perspectives on the pastoral role adopted by academics, and considers how we ensure we provide appropriate support whilst maintaining our boundaries. Despite the usefulness of knowing what students think our responsibilities are, this needs to be balanced with any formal pastoral role you may have, the responsibilities outlined by your institution[22], and with your own workload and wellness. It is hugely beneficial to seek both support and clarity on departmental expectations from your colleagues. Additionally, although you might not have a 'formal' pastoral role often students will 'just go to academics they trust.'[23] This means it's really important to familiarise yourself with the pastoral support systems at your institution, as well as good practice for when you have an unexpected visit from a student.

Despite the likelihood of students approaching us with their concerns, they were aware we can't always 'solve' them. Indeed, a number of participants were aware we might only be able to 'signpost.' This is likely reassuring for those of us who might feel we should be able to do more. The most important thing we can do is to listen to their concerns, and to make sure we have the knowledge about 'what services are available and how to access those services'

---

[21] Gareth Hughes (et al), 'Student mental health: The role of academics' (Student Minds, 2018), available at: studentminds.org.uk/uploads/3/7/8/4/3784584/180129_student_mental_health__the_role_and_experience_of_academics__student_minds_pdf.pdf (accessed 2 October 2023); On the role of academics see ch 2.

[22] Cf. Bruce MacFarlane, *The Academic Citizen: The Virtue of Service in University Life* (Routledge, 2007) 70 on the 'invisible' nature of pastoral care; see also Margaret McAllister (et al), 'Staff experiences of providing support to students who are managing mental health challenges: A qualitative study from two Australian universities' (2014) 12(3) Advances in Mental Health 192, 196 on the nature of pastoral care as a 'significant, but nor formally recognised' element of academic work. See also Chapter 6.

[23] See generally, Advance HE, *Understanding Adjustments: Supporting Staff and Students Who Are Experiencing Mental Health Difficulties*, available at: advance-he.ac.uk/knowledge-hub/understanding-adjustments-supporting-staff-and-students-who-are-experiencing-mental (accessed 2 October 2023).

so they can engage with the appropriate support, and we can be confident they have been referred appropriately.

However, even where we can't personally deal with a particular issue what is important is that we show empathy:[24]

> It makes things really difficult if they don't care ... one of the things that makes academic and pastoral support effective ... is that you care enough to establish relationships and get to know people. If you just don't care, it is going to be generic.

In contrast:

> If they are empathetic, if they are actively listening and actually understanding what you are telling them, you know, then [it shows that they care and it's easier to talk to them] ... they need to care in order to help you and support you, they have to care about your situation and listen and pay attention.

Again, this emphasises the importance of adopting a personal approach, listening, and relationship building.[25]

In addition to providing a space where students can talk, and where we listen, some of the more specific examples used by participants that indicated academics genuinely care about their students included: checking-in; asking about things raised in previous conversations; getting in touch after exams; congratulating students on their achievements; and attending their graduation ceremonies. This assists in building a positive staff-student relationship.[26] Further to this, one of the ways we can show we care, and increase students' awareness of the support on offer, is to be proactive rather than waiting for students to approach us. Whether this is by sending your advisees an email inviting them to chat, or reminding students during a teaching session that you're there to provide support, or even signposting other sources of support, these small steps can be useful.

---

[24] Jacquelin Mackinnon, 'Academic Supervision: Seeking Metaphors and Models for Quality' (2004) 28(4) Journal of Further and Higher Education 395–405.

[25] See also Chapters 5, 6, 8 and 11.

[26] On the importance of 'care' and building positive staff-student relationships see e.g., Amanda Hayes, *Teaching Adults* (Continuum International, 2006).

4.5 BARRIERS TO EFFECTIVE PASTORAL SUPPORT

4.5.1 Emphasis on Students Reaching Out

As we saw in response to the discussion on effective pastoral support, academics being proactive and shifting the 'burden' of reaching out was essential in encouraging students to reach out and demonstrating we care. Similar themes emerged when discussing the barriers faced by students when seeking support:

> The university expects us to go to them, but ... it's very difficult to reach out ... and if you don't ask for help, then nobody knows what's going on.

One of the reasons students can be reluctant to reach out for support is due to the stigma associated with many of the factors that may lead a student to require pastoral support:[27]

> The thing is we as students we know it's there [pastoral support], but it's like the stigma ... it's hard on us.

Even when directly asked whether they needed support, or whether there was anything impacting their studies students can be reluctant to disclose:

> I would always answer no. I don't have any difficulties. I thought this is my problem, my circumstances, my choices in life ... I put it all on me ... I don't want to take advantage of this system. I don't want to receive extra help. I want to do it on my own like my colleagues. I don't want to get ... preferential treatment.

For those students who don't feel comfortable reaching out, or don't know who to reach out to, having us take those first steps opens up a range of support opportunities for them and allows us to reassure them. If we notice, for example, a student's attendance is dropping, or they participate less in class, or arrive late, gently enquiring about whether a student needs any support helps to start this process. They may not disclose the barriers they are facing straight away but knowing you care and are there to help makes it more likely they will, when they're ready, approach you for support or guidance about where to go next.

There were several suggestions as to how we can play a more active role in encouraging students to make us aware of what support they need or any con-

---

[27] On 'stigma' see e.g., Walker (n 14) 310, 315; Eccles et al (n 14) 191–208.

cerns they have. First was that it would be useful if academics/departmental support teams:

> reached out to us before exams ... at least once, letting us know that they're there, or even like during the year ... [to say] 'just a wellbeing check', 'just checking on you', 'if you need anything we're here'.

Second was it would be useful for those who have personal tutor/academic advisor role to:

> Explicitly ask you how you're doing emotionally. 'How is this going?', 'Last time you told me about this'. I don't wanna say they have to be therapist or anything ... But having that scheduled conversation with somebody really, really helped and a lot of students who would have never reached out on their own.

This would help students feel more comfortable opening up about their experiences.

When faced with large numbers of students, this personalised approach (and remembering all the necessary information) can prove difficult. Scheduling time to make notes after meeting with a student, and to revisit those notes before your next meeting, can be really useful. It's also helpful to familiarise yourself with assessment deadlines and where your students are in their degree cycle so you can check in with them during potentially stressful periods. In addition, sometimes adopting a personalised approach does not require us to remember everything, but rather to adopt a welcoming and caring tone. Indeed, memorisation is not personalisation; students are generous with their expectations of your powers of recall. They are looking for you to be personal in the moment. For example, rather than responding to an email in a mechanical or matter of fact matter, little things like wishing them well with an assessment, reminding them to take break from their studies, or asking them how their summer was shows we have an interest in them as people.

Additionally the usefulness of having a specific, scheduled time to meet outside of 'open door' policy/office hours was also emphasised by other participants.[28] They also thought it would be useful to explicitly frame these sessions as linked to wellness 'so people know if that's what they're going to get,' lessening some of the uncertainty that often prevents students from

---

[28] It is also of note that when using 'office hours' it is useful to outline what these involve and what the benefits of engaging with office hours are for students, subject to departmental policies and expectations. Cf. Margaret Smith et al, '"Office Hours are Kind of Weird": Reclaiming a Resource to Foster Student-Faculty Interaction' (2017) 12 InSight 14–29.

reaching out.[29] When inviting students to these sessions, or when directing students to your office hours we can take this opportunity to outline what they are for. Scheduling these sessions can also assist in building relationships with students which in turn helps us to notice when students might be struggling. Often students won't realise they need help until someone external raises this as a possibility, or they reach crisis point and require immediate support:

> I was really unwell. I didn't realise it. I didn't know ... I felt like I wasn't doing well in any aspect. I felt like my university grades were dropping. My work performance was lower ... But in the end, my story, is a happy story ... I'm really happy that I got some support because otherwise I don't think I would have made it.

4.5.2 'Friendly' Competition Amongst Law Students

Relationship building is an integral part of creating an environment that can lessen some of the factors leading to students requiring pastoral support (for example: stress, loneliness, isolation, perceptions of academic inability). It also helps to create an environment where students feel more comfortable reaching out for help, and so students are more likely to be aware of, and access, the support they need. Relationship building is important not only between staff and students as discussed above, but also between students themselves. However, the 'competitive' nature of law school can prevent students from seeking the support of their peers, or that provided by the department/ university:[30]

> You always feel like you're in competition with your peers ... trying to balance your mental health, trying to do better than everybody. It's a huge amount of pressure.

This feeling that they need to out-perform their peers means students can find it difficult to build an informal support network amongst their friends, because they don't want to be perceived as someone that is struggling, that doesn't have what it takes to be a lawyer. This 'fear of failure' can have a negative impact on student mental health and wellness and increase their need for pastoral support.[31] We have the ability to reframe this. When students talk about the

---

[29] Fiona Donson and Catherine O'Sullivan, 'Building Block or Stumbling Block? Teaching Actus Reus and Mens Rea in Criminal Law' in Kris Gledhill and Ben Livings (eds), *The Teaching of Criminal Law: The Pedagogical Imperatives* (Routledge, 2016) 7.

[30] See also Chapters 5 and 10.

[31] See Craig Thorley, 'Not by Degrees: Improving Student Mental Health in the UK's Universities' (Institute of Public Policy Research, 2017), available at: ippr.org/files/2017-09/1504645674_not-by-degrees-170905.pdf (accessed 2 October 2023).

competition, fear of failing, and their concerns about supportive measures giving them an 'advantage,' it's important we explain why for example, an extension or mitigating circumstances are not providing them with an advantage or 'preferential treatment' but instead are intended to 'even out the playing field'. Additionally, we can also draw on our own experience of collaborative working, and the importance placed on teamwork in law firms etc.

Activities aimed at community building were indicated as being really useful in providing pastoral support.[32] This is something we can build into our teaching practice.

We can encourage collaboration/relationship building in the classroom and build activities (and an accompanying narrative) that shows students' peer-relationships are hugely beneficial. This helps us to begin to dismantle the idea they are all in competition. For example, we can encourage collaborative seminar preparation whether this is through suggesting pre-seminar discussion or research sessions, or providing them with a collaborative online space. We can also include activities based on teamwork within seminars and workshops such as negotiations, collaborative posters/presentations, or think-pair-share. Encouraging students to build peer relationships can also result in a cascade of support and advice through student communities and can help to reduce some of the stigma surrounding so many of the barriers students face.

4.5.3 Who Fills 'The Gap'

One of the most significant barriers in seeking support, particularly in relation to mental health, was the significant waiting lists for counselling and therapy both provided by the university and other alternatives. One of the participants reflected on their experience with mental health service at their university:

> They were basically like it's full ... The alternative was ... if you were like on the verge of [attempting] suicide. That's the only way that they would have found time to see you. Which I thought was really jarring. I was like, ok, well, so there's actually nothing I can do for myself.

This gap in provision has meant those who are not in pastoral services/roles are increasingly a source of this support, and it can add to the pressure we might feel to fill this gap particularly when we are new to our role.[33] We might even remember how it felt to be a student taking the huge step of reaching out to

---

[32] On the role of community in promoting positive mental health and wellness see James Duffy, Rachael Field and Melinda Shirley, 'Engaging Law Students to Promote Psychological Health' (2011) 36 Alternative Law Journal 250; and Chapter 7.
[33] See also Chapter 10.

be met with perceived indifference, or to have reached out and found a lack of support. However, we only have very minimal training, and are not in a position to provide adequate mental health support (notwithstanding the significant impact this can have on both our workload and wellness). Given that:

> students do go up to the lecturers and say I'm feeling this, I'm feeling that. And ... they can recognize when a student is maybe not having the best time and maybe need some more support than they're getting.

We need to ensure we access training where it is available, or advocate for provision where it is not. Academics find themselves on the 'frontline' and so we 'need to be equipped and enabled to respond appropriately to students in need.'[34] Given our student-facing roles we are both a first point of call for many students, but we're also in a position to notice students needing support who 'don't go to the tutors' when problems arise. Accessing support and training ourselves ensures we feel more comfortable and able to provide appropriate support. Further, this also responds to the concerns raised by participants about keeping the academic and pastoral separate.

One of the concerns colleagues often raise about providing pastoral support is the pressure it can place on our time, and the impact it can have on our own mental health and wellness.[35] Participants were also keen to emphasise it's important that:

> the person that is giving support is being supported themselves, especially in academia, because it's such a high pressure, tense situation all the time. So many deadlines.

The emotional strain in providing, or being unable to provide, the support students need and the huge pressures on our time can be overwhelming. However, students know we 'don't have time' and need 'support.' They understand we're 'human too.' With this in mind, the best thing we can do is seek out support when we need it, and signpost students when something goes beyond our expertise. It can often feel like we're letting them down, but students really do understand our limitations, perhaps better than we do sometimes.

---

[34] McAllister et al (n 22) 192, 192.
[35] On the wellbeing of academic staff in UK Law Schools see: Clare Wilson and Caroline Strevens, 'Perceptions of psychological well-being in UK law academics' (2018) 52(3) The Law Teacher 335–49.

4.6 THE LINK BETWEEN PASTORAL AND ACADEMIC

Despite the potential difficulties we face when providing pastoral support, participants emphasised the important role this can have in bringing together academic support and pastoral support rather than keeping them 'completely separate.' Where we can offer pastoral and academic support, we're able to see the connections between the academic and the pastoral:

> They can understand the nuances behind your behaviour or work or why you've missed one or two lessons. And then they're going to be in a better position to offer you better support.

When asked about the links between academic performance/attainment and pastoral support/wellness, the majority of participants saw a very clear link between the two:

> I've noticed with myself that when I feel my best, I do best and when I feel worse, I procrastinate. I wait until the very last moment and I rush it and then I feel guilty. It's just a whole cycle and it's just not great.

This echoes the links between academic attainment/performance and mental health and wellness.[36]

However, it is important to note that often, even where students recognise they are struggling, external pressure and cultural expectations may make them feel like this is not something that can be prioritised:

> I have to achieve certain things. I'm Asian, so I have some certain expectations and it doesn't really matter. My mental health. I just have to power through and achieve.

---

[36] Both 'academic and pastoral support is an integral part of the student's learning experience' Cahill et al (n 19) 398, 398. See also: Phil Topham and Naomi Moller, 'New Students' Psychological well-being and its relation to first year academic performance in a UK university' (2011) 11(3) Counselling and Psychology Research 196–203; Ward Struthers (et al), 'An examination of the relationship among academic stress, coping motivation and performance in college' (2000) 41(5) Research in Higher Education, 581–92; Ann-Marie Houghton and Jill Anderson, 'Embedding Mental Wellbeing in the Curriculum: Maximising Success in Higher Education' (HEA, 2017), available at: advance-he.ac.uk/knowledge-hub/embedding-mental-wellbeing-curriculum-maximising-success-higher-education (accessed 2 October 2023).

As such we need to ensure we recognise the diversity of student experience and acknowledge the wider context of their studies.[37] The additional pressure, expectations, or stigma experienced by students can make them even more reluctant to disclose issues. This emphasises the importance of integrating pastoral support in the classroom and every-day practice.[38] Doing so normalises and de-stigmatises seeking pastoral support and allows us to communicate the support available to students en masse rather than individually. It can also be useful to remind students that accessing support will not be disclosed to employers, or family members, nor will it appear on their transcript. Outlining the benefits pastoral support can have on their academic attainment can also be reassuring.

In addition to adopting some of the approaches outlined above, there are other steps we can take in our academic role to provide pastoral support:

> When a student has been encouraged to feel good about a certain module ... told 'Good luck everybody, I hope you guys do well.' I just think morale really helps performance.

We all want our students to do well, and though it might seem obvious, they want to hear it too! It can help students feel more confident in their own abilities, but also more comfortable reaching out if they do need additional support.

The pastoral-academic relationship does not only work in one direction but is instead cyclical. The negative 'spiral' that can emerge in relation to students' mental health and wellness can arise due to perceptions of academic attainment/achievement, or from perceived or 'actual' poor performance.[39] One of the participants reflected on some of the discussions they have observed during their time at law school:

> I'm only getting a 'B'... there's like kind of that kind of culture a lot of the time in academia that if you're not getting those 'A' grades then what's the point ...

This pressure to attain top grades is something we need to recognise and acknowledge when supporting students. We can normalise not 'always' getting 'good' grades by sharing our own experiences. For example, I fre-

---

[37] See e.g., Jason Arday, 'Understanding Mental Health: What Are the Issues for Black and Ethnic Minority Students at University?' (2018) 7(10) Social Sciences 196; Nicola Frampton et al., 'Understanding Student Mental Health Inequalities: International Students', available at: studentminds.org.uk/mh-inequalities-international-students.html (accessed 2 October 2023). See also Chapters 3 and 8.

[38] See also Chapter 9.

[39] Ann L Lijima, 'Lessons Learned: Legal Education and Law Student Dysfunction' (1998) 48 Journal of Legal Education 524, 527.

quently talk about my abysmal public law grade and how despite feeling like this was the end of the world, or at least my degree, it wasn't. It has become a really useful way of reassuring students that even academics didn't get a First in every subject (or perhaps that's just me). We can also remind students that learning is a process and there will inevitably be certain modules or topics we excel in, and others that are more challenging, and this will be different for everyone. It can also be helpful to remind them their grade is not a reflection of their ability overall but rather just what was submitted here and offer/signpost help with building on the feedback they have received.

4.7 CONCLUSION

The views collected during the focus groups demonstrate student perspectives on, and experiences of, pastoral provision are varied. However, there are themes running through these diverse perspectives that allow us to reflect on how we, and the sector more broadly, might adapt our practice so as to more effectively meet the needs of students. Pastoral support needs to be wide ranging, and personal. Central to this was the importance of relationship building and community both peer-to-peer and staff-student. Where students approach us, it is essential we are able to respond with empathy, but that we also recognise our own limitations. Listening and signposting are, as the participants emphasised, 'enough.' To provide the best support for your students, you also need that support. There was also an emphasis on the connection between academic attainment and pastoral support. On one hand this is why many students approach those who do not have a formal pastoral role, but it also provides us with an opportunity to acknowledge this link in our practice. Though many of the changes needed are beyond our control, as academics there are steps we can take, based on student views, to improve their experience of law school.

4.8 SUMMARY

1. Pastoral support encompasses a wide range of factors for students. What brings all this together is 'care.' We have an important part to play, ensuring we acknowledge the 'personal' nature of many pastoral concerns. However, we can't 'fix' everything. More importantly, students don't expect us to.
2. Understand and accept the limitations of the support you can offer. Making sure we seek guidance from colleagues on when and where we should signpost can help us set appropriate boundaries, while making sure students are able to access the support they need.

3. Listening to students, and relationship building (both staff-student and peer), are essential in creating an environment where students are more willing to reach out for help and where we can notice when students may need support. It can also lessen the need for intervention/escalation in some cases.
4. The link between academic attainment and pastoral support means we should consider how one might impact the other when offering guidance and advice.

5. Supporting law students: student support officers' perspectives

Lydia Bleasdale, Max Broady, Charlotte Guest, James Johnston

So far, you've heard from individuals writing about student support from their perspectives and providing suggestions for how you might approach the support you give to your students. Many of those chapters have made passing or more detailed references to student support officers and/or processes within their institutions. The interview in this chapter puts the experiences of three student support officers at the School of Law, University of Leeds, front and centre. (Please note that the officers' initials have been used throughout the interview to identify them.)

As context for the discussion: the School of Law at Leeds sits within the Faculty of Social Sciences (made up of a number of Schools). The law school has dedicated student support officers whose roles relate entirely to pastoral care for School of Law students (including assessment extensions, mitigating circumstances, disability support, referrals to other centralised services such as student counselling, and personal tutoring allocations). The structure and processes of each university can vary enormously: your own place of work, for example, might not have officers whose roles relate only to School of Law students, or you might not have any student support officers at all. You must ensure you're familiar with its structures and processes. Hopefully, whatever your specific circumstances, this interview with three colleagues with extensive experience of supporting a range of students will help you within your role(s). So, onto our questions …

5.1 WHAT ARE THE MOST COMMON WELLBEING ISSUES STUDENTS APPROACH YOU ABOUT IN YOUR ROLE?

MB: Mental health, certainly. Specifically, anxiety and depression.[1] These issues tend to be ongoing so when a student presents with mental health issues, we will often see them repeatedly throughout their degree. Physical health, but these issues are less often recurring. Family ill health, bereavement, caring responsibilities, financial issues or balancing studies and paid employment, disability [are other issues we might see].

CG: Mental health is definitely the biggest wellbeing issue we deal with. I have also had some students disclose wellbeing issues related to sexual assault and drink spiking.[2]

JJ: Mental health is often an all-encompassing reason why students will approach me for support, as these issues are often impacting on their ability to study and creating barriers to engagement. Students will also present wellbeing and support-related issues to me that are compounding their present situation and contributing to a feeling of low self-worth (if, for example, they are not able to access suitable disability support without a formal diagnosis or evidence of a support need).

5.2 HAVE THOSE ISSUES CHANGED OVER TIME SINCE YOU HAVE BEEN IN THIS TYPE OF ROLE AND, IF SO, HOW? WHY DO YOU THINK ANY CHANGES HAVE OCCURRED?

MB: It's a little hard to say as we have so many more students than when I started, but I am sure we see more mental health issues and more students asking about disability support. I assume this reflects a positive change in culture where society is more open about discussing mental health issues

---

[1] The Student Experiences Insight Survey (2021) suggests that this represents the national picture, available at: ons.gov.uk/peoplepopulationandcommunity/healthandsocialcare/healthandwellbeing/bulletins/coronavirusandfirstyearhighereducationstudentsengland/4octoberto11october2021 (accessed 2 October 2023).

[2] This interview was conducted in the first term of the 2021/22 academic year, when drink spiking was receiving national attention.

and more likely to seek support for a disability. Sadly, I have definitely seen a rise in the reporting of sexual assaults. Again, this is likely to be at least partly a result of people being more empowered to report these occurrences – I'm sure the #metoo movement has had an effect.

JJ: Like Max, I'm aware of more students reaching out for disability support connected to their mental health and I'm conscious there's a stronger awareness for students to 'do something' about their mental health at university, whether that's talking to someone who can help and/or seeking a formal diagnosis from their GP. I've noticed a significant increase in students registering with [the university's] Disability Services for additional support, and we've had increasing numbers of students registering as disabled owing to a mental health condition. I think there's greater awareness of disability support within the school/university.

More specifically on disability needs, I have noticed an increase in students identifying with a neurodiverse condition, such as ADHD and Autism. Although many have had to undergo costly assessments for their diagnosis, they are responding well (as a collective) to the formalised and specialist support available and willing to advocate for themselves to staff and students.

There are also significant changes I've experienced and been involved in through the provision of more localised disability peer-support, which has provided a space for discussion and navigation of mental health support within the school/university. This is something I've helped many students set-up because they've wanted to feel more connected to other students with disabilities, as opposed to navigating this individually.

5.3 WHAT DO YOU ANTICIPATE BEING THE MOST COMMON WELLBEING ISSUES STUDENTS WILL EXPERIENCE OVER THE NEXT FIVE TO TEN YEARS?

MB: More of the same! I expect more financial hardship and more anxiety associated with a more pressurised job market.

JJ: Yes, like Max I think the concerns of financial hardship and pressures of succeeding in a highly competitive graduate role will antagonise student mental health and create wellbeing issues. I think an increasing number of students, particularly those from widening participation[3] backgrounds, will

---

[3] Also known as first generation or underrepresented students.

be facing marginalised representation of their needs and access to support in years to come, due to a potential lack of financial support available within universities and generally not being able to afford the extra costs of a disability assessment or formal diagnosis at university.

5.4 I WONDER IF YOU HAVE ANY REFLECTIONS ON HOW TO SUPPORT THE WELLBEING OF INTERNATIONAL STUDENTS IN PARTICULAR? OR DO YOU THINK THE TERM 'INTERNATIONAL' COVERS SO MANY DIVERSE GROUPS OF PEOPLE, AND INDIVIDUALS, THAT IT WOULD BE HARD TO SAY THERE ARE SPECIFIC ISSUES WHICH ALL, OR MOST, INTERNATIONAL STUDENTS EXPERIENCE?[4]

MB: It's not always helpful to think of international students as a group with distinct or different issues. So many of the issues students present with are universal. I do think that when it comes to supporting international students the emphasis is always on 'what can the international students do to fit in?' rather than, 'what can Home students do to make international students feel more welcome?.'[5]

CG: I echo what Max has said – homesickness, financial hardship, etc. are common among both Home and international students. The only wellbeing issues pertaining to international students tend to surround language/cultural barriers and social isolation as a consequence. However, this is only a select group of students and some international students have no issues integrating, even when English is not their first language.

JJ: I think there are some significant cultural differences in how some international students fit into UK higher education compared to how UK students do so themselves. Language barriers can be a factor and often create wellbeing related issues for those students who struggle to communicate during

---

[4] Cf. Rachael O'Connor, '"It makes me feel empowered and that we can make a difference": Reverse mentoring between international students and staff in legal education' (2022) 3(1) European Journal of Legal Education 95–126, where the visibility of, and challenges experienced by, international students are discussed.

[5] See also Chapter 2.

social interaction and teaching activities, because they can be put on the spot to practice their English listening and speaking skills at the same time. I see some students who will hone in on groups of students from the same background across campus and more locally when participating in wellbeing or social activities, such as our school wellbeing activities. They seem to feel more comfortable expressing themselves with students from their own country or nationality, and I guess many domestic students just accept this, rather than trying to join an international student group themselves.

From a wellbeing perspective, I've found many to be able to communicate very confidently over email or through MS Teams, as opposed to in-person. As a former international student myself, I found it fascinating to witness home US students refer to me as 'European' when I had always identified as a 'UK student' and despite my national identity being a minority in the group of international (English speaking) students I associated with. From this perspective I do agree Home (UK students) could do more to make international students fit in to UK universities and not so much take it for granted that international students will be able to adapt to the student experience like others do.

There are specific issues international students can face at university [when accessing student support], which can be barriers to engagement. For example, international students whose diagnosis of a specific learning difficulty or impairment in their home country, may not correlate to a recognised diagnosis in the UK. This can prevent them from accessing appropriate disability support for their needs. As an international student who is trying to access formalised and specialist support for a diagnosis or learning impairment, they firstly need to be assessed to see if they qualify for any disability related funding via their home country or a sponsor.

5.5 DO YOU THINK THE ISSUES YOU MOST COMMONLY SEE ARE SPECIFIC TO LAW STUDENTS, OR DO YOU THINK THEY'RE UNIVERSAL?

MB: Again, I'd say the majority are universal, but there are some specific traits. I think Law students tend to see *themselves* as different – I've often heard them say it's a particularly difficult degree, and have heard them contrast it with what they perceive to be less demanding subjects. I do think they are a particularly competitive group. They see their peers as their rivals rather than colleagues, competing for the same jobs, vacation schemes, etc. They sometimes perhaps miss an opportunity to support each other as much as they could. I think some students still see Law as a discipline dominated by people from white and privileged backgrounds, and students with different backgrounds can feel they do not 'fit in'. We also see a lot of high achievers who struggle with what they perceive to be failure. They perhaps were straight-A pupils at school and then they come here and 'only' get 62 on their level one assessments, and for many it is the first time they are not top of their class. They see this as a failure and find it hard to come to terms with. Lastly, some of the additional or extra-curricular course costs for Law – buying a suit, travelling to London – can cause issues.

CG: I too find Law students can have specific traits, in particular thinking that asking for help may be a sign of 'weakness'; leaving workloads to become unmanageable before asking for support; generally thinking they have to and should be doing everything on their own. I think this is, as Max says, due to their competitive and perfectionist traits.

JJ: Absolutely, there are indeed competitive and perfectionist traits in Law students and I think these are the areas they need to pay more attention to for their own personal development and leadership qualities. I feel like I work in an inclusive community where mental health and wellbeing is considered, and supported, for those who have a strong desire to succeed and perform. But I come across many Law students selling themselves aggressively on LinkedIn, who overlook what it means to be a part of an inclusive community and how this can really help them develop as a professional and diversify some of their employability skills. The imposter syndrome I believe is fuelled by this culture of competitive and perfectionist Law students – who may see themselves as confident to speak out in seminars and leaders of group activity – but this unfortunately creates an unsupportive experience for many other students.[6]

5.6 WHY DO YOU THINK SOME STUDENTS DON'T APPROACH A TUTOR, OR A STUDENT SUPPORT OFFICER, UNTIL AN ISSUE BECOMES COMPLETELY OVERWHELMING FOR THEM?[7]

CG: I think some students feel asking for help is a sign of failure. They put pressure on themselves to do it alone and it gets to a point where they can no longer do this.

MB: Absolutely agree. I also think, with mental health issues, they can slowly develop over weeks and months and a student might only realise or accept

---

[6] See also Chapters 2, 4 and 11.
[7] See also Chapters 3, 9, 10 and 11.

they are not coping when they, for instance, fail to submit an essay (compared with, say, a broken wrist where they would most likely reach out for support immediately).

JJ: Contrary to Max and Charlotte's views here I do think students, particularly disabled students with a mental health diagnosis, approach a tutor or student support officer regarding support before the issue becomes overwhelming. But I think that's because disabled students have a better understanding of what a structure for support looks like, including how it can be communicated to their tutors and how it can benefit them.

They are rarely in a position in which asking for support is the result of an issue they've put off doing something about for some time and more because they're in the position of not receiving the support they're entitled to. Disability support has allowed students over time to generally change their understanding regarding asking for help and communicating their circumstances. However, I do agree – especially with Law students – that many deem asking for help as a weakness or sign of failure. Like all student communities, there are always going to be factors preventing engagement or proactiveness, no matter how hard you try to communicate the message of asking for help and when and where to do that.

5.7 FROM YOUR CONVERSATIONS WITH STUDENTS, WHY DO YOU THINK SOME OF THEM FEEL MORE ABLE TO APPROACH STUDENT SUPPORT OFFICERS ABOUT WELLBEING MATTERS THAN THEIR TUTORS?

CG: I think students may view the two roles as distinct and separate: personal tutors deal with academic support, student support deal with pastoral support. In reality, both need to work closely together to offer the optimum support to the student.[8] Students may also be more likely to approach student support as they need someone who is 'outside' of the situation. I have many students come to me to discuss personal issues which they don't want personal tutors to be aware of. They may feel embarrassed or worried about disclosing this information and whether it will remain private/confidential. Because our role is specifically designed to offer this support, they feel like there are clearer boundaries and expectations; this makes them feel more at ease.

---

[8] See also Chapter 11.

MB: I agree students often do not want their teaching staff to be aware of the issues they are facing. I think they feel they might be letting them down. We obviously try to disabuse them of this notion!

JJ: There is a distinction in what student support officers can offer compared to academics, but the need for coordinated support and to make this more visible is crucial for the student experience. I think it often depends on the relationship a student can form with their tutors and how they perceive what boundaries are being communicated to them, as to how comfortable they will feel discussing wellbeing matters. Sometimes students just want the person they've decided to speak to, to listen and discuss their matters with them rather than be signposted onto someone else or a service where they may have to go through a formal disclosure. If a student has perhaps understood from speaking with other students or staff that a student support officer will do that, this can be one reason why student support officers are approached first.

5.8 IMAGINE YOU HAD AN ACADEMIC COLLEAGUE WHO WAS EARLY ON IN THEIR CAREER ASKING FOR HINTS AND TIPS ABOUT HOW TO ENSURE STUDENTS FELT ABLE TO APPROACH THEM ABOUT WELLBEING MATTERS. WHAT WOULD YOU SAY TO THEM?

CG: I would say try to make yourself visible/available at regular intervals, check-in with students, outline your role and the kinds of support you can offer. Often students don't want to approach people about issues because they feel others are too busy or this isn't their remit. Clarifying support and making it easily accessible is the best way to engage tutees.

MB: I think it really helps when academic staff show a bit of their personal side and, yes, perhaps even some of their weakness.[9] Students can see academic staff as these infallible, unflappable role models which is an impossible expectation to live up to. But I think it makes a difference if academics can pull back the curtain and let students in a bit – reveal, say, that they were rejected for 20 jobs before they started at Leeds, or that they struggled with

---

[9] See also Chapters 4 and 8.

certain aspects of the pandemic. By sharing something like this they can build trust, humanise (there must be a better word than that!) the role of the academic, and make themselves seem more approachable.

JJ: Providing some transparency in communicating how easy it is for a student to connect with you and how approachable you are, will help a student understand there are little to no barriers for them to engage with you. Play to your strengths regarding what you would feel most comfortable discussing with a student and what you know you can help with through your own skills and experience towards student wellbeing.

5.9 HOW CAN ACADEMIC COLLEAGUES, INCLUDING THOSE EARLY ON IN THEIR CAREER, HELP TO SUPPORT YOU IN YOUR ROLES?

CG: I think a better understanding of our role by academic colleagues would help. Student support is such a broad term but what we can offer is fairly specific – to meet with students and listen to their problems, signpost them to appropriate support services, and advise them on mitigation procedures for assessments. Oftentimes we are seen as the team that can help with any general student enquiries and this isn't really our role. I also think academic colleagues should be clear about their own boundaries in the role and what they can/cannot provide support with.

MB: Also, communication between the two teams. Obviously, we respect the students' confidentiality, but when they are happy to share it's best for the student if everyone is aware what's going on. I would also encourage academic staff to maintain the boundaries of the role for everyone's benefit. Academic staff can cause problems if they over-promise or wrongly advise students on mitigating circumstances applications. Academics should also remember they are not counsellors – nor are the student support officers! – so the student/staff relationship should not veer into that kind of territory. I know this only ever comes from a place of wanting to help, but there are dedicated and appropriately trained counsellors available.

JJ: The opportunity to share and develop an awareness of our role with academics is a must for me, as I believe that will not only strengthen communication, but also allow for a stronger understanding of how we can work together. I recognise the strength and value academic advice can bring to any student support issue or meeting where mental health and wellbeing is being discussed, because the student is usually in a position where they will need to make an informed decision for themselves, to move forward and access appropriate support in a university setting.

5.10 WHAT DO YOU THINK THE IDEAL RELATIONSHIP SHOULD BE BETWEEN PERSONAL TUTORS OR OTHER ACADEMIC COLLEAGUES, STUDENT SUPPORT OFFICERS, UNIVERSITY SUPPORT SYSTEMS (SUCH AS CENTRAL COUNSELLING SERVICES), AND WELLBEING SUPPORT WITHIN THE COMMUNITY (SUCH AS THROUGH NHS SERVICES)?

CG: That's a tough question and I'm not sure if there is an ideal relationship. I would say, from previous experience, close contact between personal tutors and student support officers is important. Students tend to benefit most from this close relationship because the personal tutor, student support officer and student are able to create a plan of action and regularly check-in. The plan can be informed from relevant angles, in particular, the student's academic progress and support, as well as supporting their emotional wellbeing and whatever circumstances they may be dealing with in their life. I would say strong links with student support officers and the university support systems are important but at present they seem slightly disconnected. We refer students to them and receive supporting evidence for mitigation cases, but do not have any further engagement. In terms of support from external providers, I think it is much more difficult to achieve continuity. NHS services such as counselling have incredibly long waiting lists and I would always refer students to the university counselling services in the first instance. I often do refer students to discuss support with their GP although this is usually to support mental health concerns and medication.

MB: I think there is value in student support officers being located and embedded within a School, not just for the programme-specific knowledge they obtain (I've been here nearly nine years and still have to look things up about the curricula or progression and classification rules) but also for strengthening their relationship with academic colleagues.[10] You occa-

---

[10] Lydia Bleasdale and Sarah Humphreys, *Undergraduate Resilience Research Project* (LITE; University of Leeds, 2019).

sionally hear rumours from senior management about centralising student support services but I think a lot more would be lost than could possibly be gained.

JJ: An ideal relationship to me would see strong teamwork with colleagues in the school and relevant services in the university and for the purposes of delivering localised/targeted supported to students in the school. I think we can do that very well for law and criminology students, with having strong programme-specific knowledge of these disciplines, an awareness of the taught activities and assessments, and being able to articulate this with the guidance and practical support mechanisms we're familiar with (that often rely on us utilising relationships with academics). Because of student confidentiality, it can be difficult to construct an ideal relationship with wider university support and external services. Most of the time we are essentially sign-positing students to these services, before expecting them to independently explore the support and guidance themselves.

5.11 YOU ALL WORK WITH STUDENTS WHO ARE POTENTIALLY EMOTIONAL, AND EXPERIENCING CHALLENGING CIRCUMSTANCES, EVERY DAY. HOW DO YOU CREATE A BOUNDARY BETWEEN YOUR WORK AND HOME LIFE, AND HOW DO YOU THINK OTHERS (INCLUDING ACADEMIC COLLEAGUES) SHOULD DO THE SAME?

CG: I create boundaries between my work and home life by ensuring I have followed up with students over email the same day as their meeting. I think it is important not to have your emails come through your phone as this blurs the work-home divide. It stops you from potentially reading something upsetting whilst you aren't meant to be at work. I also like to take 15 mins away from my laptop if I have been in a very difficult student meeting, just to breathe, process the situation, and assess the next steps going forward.

MB: It's certainly been more difficult since working from home during the pandemic: our work life and home life sometimes occupy the same space! I think you have to be strict with yourself with the boundaries, which can be hard. We are not a crisis response service. If a student emails out of hours or at the weekend we are not expected to reply until we return to work. You have to accept the limits of your role and to accept you cannot solve all students' problems. When students have disclosed very serious issues the responsibility can feel very heavy at times, and I certainly struggled with this for quite a long time when I started. Often, we will be the first or only person they talk to about the difficulties they are facing as they do not want to tell their friends, family or teaching staff. Being there to listen and to help in whatever way I can, I recognise my role is important and can make a real difference, but I also accept I am not responsible for all the students' outcomes.

JJ: I think you have to work to your strengths, in terms of your capacity for the emotionally challenging cases you can mentally and psychologically take on in one day, and you have to work to your limits and be prepared to tell a student or staff what these limits are. As Student Support Officers, we have to trust in the university support and external services, including the digital platforms, that are there to help students out of hours or in crisis. I think every academic needs to do the same and so we are creating a can-do culture of enabling a student to independently access and explore the support they need, but follow up where necessary.[11]

5.12 THERE WILL INEVITABLY BE TIMES WHEN YOU CANNOT HELP A STUDENT AND NEED TO, FOR EXAMPLE, REFER THEM ON TO OTHER SERVICES OR TEAMS. HOW DO YOU MAINTAIN THE BOUNDARIES OF YOUR ROLE, AND WHAT ADVICE WOULD YOU HAVE FOR OTHER COLLEAGUES WHO NEED TO DO THE SAME?

CG: I think you need to be very clear with a student about the boundaries of your role and why you are referring them to specialist support services. I think giving a clear explanation of your thought processes and reasons for doing so helps them to understand the situation better.

MB: Be grateful they have felt comfortable reaching out and confiding in you, rather than berating yourself for not being able to solve all their problems. There are so many specialist support services for all the problems life throws up. Nobody could possibly be expected to do everything.

---

[11] See also Chapter 11.

JJ: I completely agree. It's often the relationship you develop with a student regarding support and guidance that will make all the difference to their willingness to move forward and engage with other people and support services. Where possible I try to facilitate an introduction between a student and relevant support services, although this isn't always possible (such as through the counselling service/mental health advisory team, where they can neither confirm nor deny a student has been in touch), but I can put trust in them responding with acknowledgment of my email (particularly if a student is at risk to themselves or others).

5.13 DO YOU FIND IT PERSONALLY AFFECTS YOU WHEN YOU CANNOT HELP A STUDENT AND, IF SO, HOW DO YOU MANAGE THAT CHALLENGE?[12]

CG: I find it can personally affect me, especially in situations where the student is subject to forces beyond their control. You almost feel like a spectator watching these circumstances unfold. That can be really difficult to deal with sometimes and I think it's important to focus on being empathetic rather than sympathetic. Sometimes it is okay to put yourself in the student's shoes and experience how they are feeling. You have to remember things change all the time and this is a just a very small phase of their life.

MB: There are two types of situations I find the hardest. Firstly, where a student is doing everything you could possibly recommend for their mental health and they are still struggling. It's hard to know what to say. I once read a remark that almost all emotional advice boils down to 'this too shall pass', but it's hard for someone to believe that when they are overwhelmed by circumstances. Again, I sometimes just fall back on the knowledge that being there to listen will help in itself, but it can be incredibly frustrating. Secondly, where a student is struggling but is doing none of the things you have recommended which you are sure would make a difference to their circumstances. Students will make decisions you might not agree with or that you think might not be in their best interests and you have to accept that.

---

[12] See also Chapter 2.

JJ: I think where specialist support is clearly needed to help a student, such as a doctor to discuss a formal diagnosis of their mental health condition or a Specialist Skills Mentor to help with their neurodevelopmental condition, I take confidence in advising a student I cannot help with this and they need to focus on engaging with specialist help and support. It's very important to demonstrate empathy but also, particularly for any student who is struggling with their mental health, to provide an opportunity to discuss a clear strategy for support they feel they can rely on beyond your engagement with them. The challenge, I feel, is that in many situations students want a reasonably quick solution or outcome to their support requirement and most of the time (from a delivery perspective), additional and specialist support does not work like that (especially if they are accessing support for the first time). Therefore, it's important to identify and encourage a 'process' the student can focus on towards accessing the support they need, and so they can commit to that – just like they would commit to any mitigating circumstances process – rather than focusing on a specific outcome or result.

5.14 SUMMARY

1. It is important to repeatedly advertise the support available to students, rather than relying on them remembering one (or even a handful) of messages about it. Students will not always remember the information if it arrived at a time when they weren't in need of it but, even if they do, students will not always be immediately willing to ask for help. This can be for a wide range of reasons, including a fear it makes them a 'failure', embarrassment, or for cultural reasons.
2. A key theme within the interview was the need for collaboration. For law students, who were described as tending more towards competitive than collaborative behaviour, this was seen by the support officers as being an important life skill and one which needs to be actively learnt. From the perspective of Self-Determination Theory (SDT, a theory of psychological wellbeing),[13] such collaboration could be linked to heightened wellbeing: SDT suggests relatedness – a feeling of connection with others – is an important tenet of positive wellbeing, so you could consider ways in which you might introduce opportunities for collaboration within your teaching or wider interactions with students. For example, you might

---

[13] Edward L. Deci and Richard M. Ryan, 'The "What" and "Why" of Goal Pursuits: Human Needs and the Self-Determination of Behavior' (2000) 11(4) Psychological Inquiry 227–68.

consider group work and collaborative games within seminars or even assessments.

For staff, it is critical to the student experience that professional services staff and academic staff communicate and collaborate within their roles: although we all have our own experiences as students to draw upon, those experiences only offer one perspective and our professional services colleagues can offer a wide variety through working with so many students on wellbeing matters. The importance and value of professional services colleagues is often underestimated, or entirely lost, within academia, and it is important not to fall into that same trap.

3. Remember that, in Max's words, you 'aren't a crisis response service'. If you're reading this text you are, presumably, interested in student support and how you can do the best possible job at it. This interest can quickly tip over into an all-consuming desire to help, which can be damaging for your own health and wellbeing, as well as not being in the best interests of your students.[14] Familiarise yourself with the sources of support available at your own workplace and don't hesitate to refer students to them. If you're concerned this makes you look uncaring, remember Charlotte's suggestion of following up with them afterwards to see how things are going, and the reference made by all three officers to the need to explain the limits of your role clearly to your student.[15]

---

[14] See further Gareth Hughes, Mehr Panjwani, Priya Tulcidas and Nicola Byrom, *Student Mental Health: The Role and Experiences of Academics* (2018), available at: studentminds.org.uk/theroleofanacademic.html (accessed 24 October 2023).

[15] See also Chapter 11.

6. Reflections on the influence of staff and student sex and gender on the provision of pastoral support

Jenny Gibbons

The early career researchers (ECRs) in law departments involved in pastoral support are a diverse group, reflective of the span of interests in a subject that interacts with a wealth of other disciplines. The group of ECRs in most law schools includes 'home grown ECRs', who transition from being the recipient to the provider of pastoral support; 'flown in ECRs', whose research expertise make them attractive to the department but who have to quickly adapt to different pastoral cultures and processes; and 'sidestep ECRs', who choose to join academia later in life following an earlier career within the legal profession. I count myself within the latter group so this chapter will be using the insights and experiences I have accumulated from this perspective to consider what can be learnt from acknowledging the sex and gender disparities in the student and staff expectations around the provision of pastoral support. It will do this by first setting out some context to the acknowledged sex and gender disparities in the legal academic environment including what are referred to here as 'trigger events', such as emotive discussions that lead on naturally from seminar content; 'kinship events', where students actively seek out support from colleagues with uniting characteristics to their own; and 'reflective events', whereby the interaction with student(s) leads to a development in the ECRs' approach to their practice. This will be followed by some reflections founded on my experience before finally setting out some ideas for strategies to manage student, colleague and department expectations in a way that – it is hoped – also supports the development of student autonomy and resilience.

6.1　SEX AND GENDER DISPARITIES IN THE LEGAL ACADEMIC ENVIRONMENT

There is insufficient space in this chapter to engage in the complicated and contentious dispute drawing distinctions between sex and gender. Instead, I will use the terms 'female' and 'woman/women' to include all those people who, when they read the Advance HE Gender Pay Gap in Higher Education reports,[1] felt individually affected (and consequently demoralised). A large number of these people may also have personal experiences that were exposed and re-lived when reading the coverage around the #MeToo movement. I am in this group. I am also a parent and a carer who has experience of working part time in the past, which are relevant factors when considering the provision of student pastoral support, as will be set out further below.

Attempting to evaluate the range of academic, teaching and pastoral roles within UK law schools is challenging, due in part to the varying approaches taken to the allocation of employment tasks within different institutions. What is evident though is that sex and gender differences continue to play a part.[2] From the most recent information collated by the Higher Education Statistics Agency (HESA), the majority (66%) of part-time academic staff are female (which in law includes many who have 'sidestepped' out of the profession) and the vast majority (72%) of professors are male.[3] In my experience these clear discrepancies in the designation of roles manifest themselves in the allocation of responsibilities. At York Law School, as at other institutions, the majority of small group teaching is undertaken by women so, for the typical student, it is female colleagues who they are most likely to get to know, and women who they tend to turn to when they need pastoral support.

The challenges for women in the legal profession is another factor that contributes to the number of people who chose to 'sidestep' out of practice and into UK law schools. According to a recent Women in Leadership in Law report published by the Law Society, women have represented more than 60% of entrants into the solicitor profession since 1990. Yet while just more than half of practising solicitors are female, women account for only 30% of partners in private practice. This fact, together with other data in the report that shows the influence of unconscious bias in day to day practice and the volume of female solicitors leaving the profession mid-career, is problematic.[4] From

---

[1] See further at: advance-he.ac.uk/guidance/equality-diversity-and-inclusion/employment-and-careers/equal-pay (accessed 2 October 2023).

[2] Cf. Jo Cahill, Jan Bowyer and Sue Murray, 'An exploration of undergraduate students' views on the effectiveness of academic and pastoral support' (2014) 56(4) Educational Research 398–411; Christine Teelken & Rosemary Deem, 'All are equal, but some are more equal than others: managerialism and gender equality in higher education in comparative perspective' (2013) 49(4) Comparative Education 520–35; Christopher Westoby, Judith Dyson, Fiona Cowdell and Tim Buescher, 'What are the barriers and facilitators to success for female academics in UK HEIs? A narrative review' (2021) 22(8) Gender and Education 1033–56.

[3] See hesa.ac.uk/ (accessed 2 October 2023).

[4] Law Society, *Influencing for Impact: The need for gender equality in the legal profession*, available at: lawsociety.org.uk/en/topics/research/women-in-leadership-in-law-report-need-for-gender-equality (accessed 2 October 2023).

recent conversations with other 'sidestep ECRs' working in law schools there is strong recognition from experience of what is referred to in the Law Society report as the 'housekeeping work'/'glory work' distinction in law firms, and other examples of sexist practice within the profession. These types of events contributed to my exit from the profession two decades ago, so it is somewhat demoralising that such patterns of behaviour are still prevalent.

6.2 REFLECTIONS FOUNDED ON PRACTICE AT YORK LAW SCHOOL

York Law School differs from the majority of universities in its approach to legal education, in that the majority of the core curriculum is delivered using a problem-based learning (PBL) model. This is a directed experiential learning approach whereby the majority of student discussions about their research into, and understanding of, specific areas of law take place in seminar sessions with fixed groups facilitated by staff recruited and trained to be PBL tutors. Within the weekly PBL cycle the students' independent research is supported by whole cohort plenary sessions delivered by subject experts, and what are referred to as interim sessions facilitated by ECRs.[5]

Following on from the observations in the section above, the vast majority of PBL tutors at York Law School are either mid to late career women who have had experience in the past of working in legal practice (referred to here as 'sidestep ECRs'), or they are 'home grown ECRs' gaining teaching experience ahead of securing an academic post. Both of these cohorts of colleagues meet the same groups of students on a regular basis and start to recognise character traits not just of individual students but of the seminar groups as distinct and recognisable entities. This can present challenges in relation to formal and informal pastoral support, as set out further below.

6.2.1 Formal and Informal Pastoral Support

The University of York has a formal pastoral support model for students utilising a college structure, with all first year students being allocated to a specific college in which to live, with the ability to access all college resources for the rest of their time as students.[6] For some, the college plays an integral part of their student experience – branded sweaters are evident, for example – whereas

---

[5] For more on the PBL approach at York, see york.ac.uk/law/ (accessed 2 October 2023).

[6] For more on the background to the College structure at York, see David Smith, 'Eric James and the "Utopianist" Campus: Biography, Policy and the Building of a New University during the 1960s' (2008) 37(1) History of Education 23–42.

others find support where needed via informal means, as explained further below.

Within this context, all first year law students are also formally allocated a specific member of staff to be their 'Personal Advisor' for the whole of their time at the law school. The allocation of Personal Advisors to students for the main three year LLB programme is done by seminar group, so colleagues are allocated a roughly equivalent number of male and female students from a range of backgrounds. For some, the individual pastoral relationship becomes really meaningful leading, for example, to regular career updates following graduation and even wedding and christening invitations. For others it is nominal at best, with patchy attendance at the termly scheduled meetings as the Personal Advisor is not regarded as any different to other colleagues with whom the student interacts. There are various factors that contribute to the strength of this relationship, with one of them being the more ad hoc personal relationships students develop with other members of staff. This can include the module leaders of optional modules, where the challenges posed by the content lends itself to more insightful conversations and disclosures, and/or the better known tutors on other core modules, including PBL.

It is evident from anecdote and experience therefore that in addition to the formal pastoral support model at York and elsewhere, an informal pastoral support model tends to emerge from conversations 'in the moment' with students, and that it is female ECRs who tend to undertake a disproportionate amount of this. For the 'sidestep ECRs' this inequity can include an uncomfortable echo of the allocation of 'housekeeping work' they experienced in practice, except that in the context of the law school the issue is not that the work they perform is unimportant but more that it is relatively undervalued when compared with the 'glory work' of academic research.

The trusting relationships that form between students and all categories of ECRs can develop from a range of circumstances including 'trigger events', such as emotive discussions that lead on naturally from seminar content, and 'kinship events', where students actively seek out support from colleagues with uniting characteristics, including race, class and/or sexuality. They can also result in 'reflective events' whereby ECRs adapt their practice as a consequence of such discussions. These will be considered in more detail below, together with suggested strategies for you to manage student, colleague and department expectations. It is acknowledged that York Law School is the environment where I have experienced the majority of my pastoral support roles, but it is evident from the extensive and insightful information in the other chapters in this book that ECRs in different institutions have similar challenges and benefit from collegiate support to enable them to address them competently.

6.3 EXAMPLES OF CHALLENGES FACED BY ECRs IN THEIR INTERACTIONS WITH STUDENTS

It is widely acknowledged that the transition from school to university is a challenging time, with lifestyle learning running alongside the academic learning events in the law school. Much has been written about this in the literature from other disciplines, most notably education and psychology, and you might have knowledge of this from prior study and/or prior experience. In my experience of working with ECRs from a range of backgrounds it is evident they understand the perspective of undergraduate students for a variety of reasons. For example, some 'home grown ECRs' and 'flown in ECRs' have familiarity with relevant theoretical content from university level training courses, including the literature on attachment theory, which informs their approaches to their interactions with students.[7] Some 'flown in ECRs' and 'sidestep ECRs' have personal experience as parents of university age children and tend to empathise with the bewilderment of the first few months especially, where students are learning to live independently at the same time as learning to perform to the different standards expected by university level education. Many 'home grown ECRs' have recent experience of involvement with seminar activities as students, making them particularly empathetic to the anxieties of students. Reflecting upon my own experience of providing pastoral support, it is evident there is an evolution in student needs and experiences over time, many of which are predictable (including the disorientation experienced by first year students at the beginning of the year, and the slump in group morale towards the end of each semester), whereas others are random events that don't fit naturally into the recognised timetable.

Set out below are a set of challenges identified from my reflections on this experience, together with some suggested approaches to assist you in adapting to your pastoral role. It is acknowledged there will be considerable difference in practice in this regard, most notably due to 'home grown ECRs' and 'flown in ECRs' experiencing a variety of administrative practice and procedure in different institutions when they were students, and 'sidestep ECRs' bringing with them a wealth of experience from alternative employment environments. The main focus here will therefore be to provide you with hypothetical examples based on a multitude of experiences and some suggested strategies to enable you to provide sufficient student support without (it is hoped) taking on a disproportionate amount of the 'housekeeping work'.

---

[7] See further e.g., John Bowlby, *A Secure Base: Clinical Applications of Attachment Theory* (Routledge, 1988).

6.3.1 An Example – the End of Lesson Chat

As set out in more detail elsewhere in this book, approachable ECR colleagues at York (of which there are many) tend to get involved in conversations at the end of teaching sessions with students who are struggling to adjust to the discursive seminar environment, or who have immediate pastoral needs. For the latter, due to the challenging subject matter of some legal scenarios, these conversations can on occasion be linked to 'trigger events' arising from classroom discussions on content including, for example, sexual offences in criminal law or different political perspectives in public law, but they can also be because the tutor is a recognisable and trusted ally.

An illustration of a challenging end of lesson chat is where a student initiates a conversation about subject coverage or tutor group dynamics, which then quickly turns into a personal disclosure. Examples of this are multiple and include conversations about anxieties associated with academic competence; coming to terms with training contract and work placement rejections; dealing with life events, such as family bereavements and the end of romantic relationships; and disclosures around a wide variety of physical and mental health issues. For women in particular there are also conversations with mature students who have specific issues relating to caring responsibilities. Although the advice to staff in these circumstances is to refer the student on to the students' personal advisor and relevant central University pastoral support, anecdotal evidence shows that colleagues tend to feel duty bound to give advice 'in the moment'. The consequence of this is that it creates an unworkloaded, and often unmentioned, responsibility to do the right thing for a large number of students across the academic year. As York, like most law schools, has a higher volume of female students and a higher proportion of women fulfilling teaching focused roles, it is women who tend to be taking on a disproportionate amount of this type of 'housekeeping' work.

These experiences are however not all negative. In addition to assisting with the development of interpersonal relationships, some of these end of lesson chats provide us with opportunities to have 'reflective events', especially when some of the (more confident) students take the opportunity to challenge us on our teaching styles and/or subject knowledge. Although this can be somewhat intimidating – and even upsetting – 'in the moment' this is an inevitable part of developing our practice as teachers so this can be a useful benefit of the end of lesson chat.

6.3.2 An Example – the Inappropriate Comment in Class

In every university classroom there will always be challenges about what are acceptable topics for discussion, and what is acceptable language to use. This is particularly true for law as a discipline as there is a requirement to discuss criminal acts and human rights violations that can act as 'trigger events' for pastoral needs depending on students' personal circumstances. I and other colleagues have discussed and analysed numerous situations in the classroom where conversations have 'taken a turn', leading to specific students becoming visibly upset or even getting up and walking out. In my human rights module seminars this has included challenging conversations about conflicting religious and cultural beliefs relating to the right to life, whereas others have mentioned how discussions about topics including sexual assault, modern slavery and the holocaust have been particularly upsetting for certain students.

This issue contributes to the debate about the extent of the concept of 'freedom' in the context of 'freedom of expression' so, in the teaching of human rights it is, of itself, an area of academic interest. There are also suggested strategies for this (discussed further below) such as the use of content warnings at the beginning of classes where contentious material will be covered to allow students the opportunity to leave the environment.[8] In some cases though, the inappropriate comment in class is not necessarily linked to the known content, meaning that the appropriate pastoral response needs to be found 'in the moment', which can be a significant source of stress for anyone new to teaching.

On occasion the inappropriate comment in class can take the form of a one-on-one argument between students where it is evident that they have had a personal relationship away from the classroom which has broken down. I have had experiences of being approached by students asking to move groups as a consequence of such events, which is challenging as it tends not to be possible for timetabling (and, in the context of PBL, pedagogical) reasons. As a consequence, I have always regarded this as a priority issue where time taken to address the matter in the moment leads to a more time effective resolution than referring students on to central university services. To do this it can be useful to explain that in the workplace you don't get to choose who you spend time with in the same way as you do at school or university, so it is essential to maintain working relationships with people despite differences in views and/or approaches to work based priorities. As with other issues around managing the classroom dynamics, it is often the ECR seminar teacher rather than the personal advisor who takes responsibility for working with the students to rebuild relationships after such events, which can take the form of an unworkloaded end of lesson chat, as explained above.

---

[8] For more on content warnings see Payton J. Jones, Benjamin W. Bellet and Richard J. McNally, 'Helping or Harming? The Effect of Trigger Warnings on Individuals with Trauma Histories' (2020) 8(5) Clinical Psychological Science 905–17.

6.3.3 An Example – the Emergency Situation

The emergency situation we might be trained to respond to – such as a student suffering from an epileptic fit in class – creates a stressful challenge, but it is one for which support is (notionally) in place via emergency phone numbers. Other emergency situations are varied, and knowing how to respond to them can be problematic as they can require an on the spot action with lasting consequences. Such events could include being the first person to be told about the death of a student's close relative, being told about a sexual assault with sufficient evidence for it to be classed as a rape, and other disclosures of events that would amount to criminal activity.

There are other situations that are not on the face of it emergency events but are regarded as such in the moment by the student involved. Examples include the failures of technology when approaching assessment deadlines, travel disruption, and – as demonstrated so strongly in recent years – the impact of global events on the students' ability to concentrate. Disclosures about these challenges can be productive but they could take an emotional toll on you, which needs to be duly recognised and supported. Suggested strategies to deal with these types of situations will be returned to below.

6.3.4 An Example – the Uniting Characteristic (Including Disability, Ethnicity, Sexuality, Gender, Life Event)

When discussing pastoral support issues with colleagues it is evident certain people take on – with varying degrees of willingness – additional responsibilities due to their own defining characteristics, or as a consequence of disclosures they have made about specific personal circumstances. For example, colleagues who disclose they have dyslexia become a magnet for students who want to discuss their own challenges with this; non-British colleagues are sought out by international students who are struggling to navigate their way around some of the cultural norms and language; some British colleagues from specific religious communities are approached for recommendations about places of worship and sources of speciality foods; and colleagues who are willing to disclose that they are members of the LGBTQ+ community are often contacted by students who are exploring their feelings about their own sexual orientation. For me, a middle-aged white woman with children, I have been happy to disclose to certain female students that I have had gynaecological issues in the past, which has led to some helpful conversations where I have advised them to seek out medical support for a range of health issues. Students from minority groups or with specific uniting characteristics clearly benefit from these types of 'kinship' conversations but it is acknowledged that some colleagues have a wariness around this as the pastoral burden is not shared equally.

As an example, it is evident that across the sector there are some people who are happy to talk about their sexuality with students, and others who include discursive content within their course materials on subjects including feminist pedagogic approaches and the rights of the LGBTQ+ community as a way to enhance the education of the student population on the issues faced by specific groups within society.[9] For this, it is generally acknowledged there is a tendency for specific colleagues to become a magnet for student approaches on the topic, leading to an additional pastoral support burden. As a consequence, it is evident that some colleagues believe their personal perspectives and/or sexuality are not relevant to their workplace identity and choose not to disclose this to students.

A worrying and ongoing issue which you might experience – in particular if you are female – is about how best to deal with ad hoc pastoral support conversations following a disclosure by female students about inappropriate sexual behaviour in student accommodation or other social settings. For as long as I have been working in the higher education environment, I and a significant number of my female colleagues have been approached about this issue, and we continue to struggle with the best way to respond. This is true both for conversations in timetabled Personal Advisor sessions and during the additional ad hoc conversations referred to above. The challenges around this issue are manifold, and there are some suggestions to assist with dealing with them below.

A final example of a uniting event relates to parenthood. It is evident that ECRs and other teaching staff who disclose that they are parents tend to get approached by students who either are parents – with all the juggling responsibility challenges that brings – or who are seeking out parental style support. As with the example above, it tends to be women who engage in these types of conversations, with the consequent workload implications.

---

[9] See further Charlotte Morris, Tamsin Hinton-Smith, Rosa Marvell and Kimberley Brayson, 'Gender back on the agenda in higher education: perspectives of academic staff in a contemporary UK case study' (2022) 31(1) Journal of Gender Studies 101–13.

6.4 SUGGESTED STRATEGIES FOR ECRs TO MANAGE STUDENT, COLLEAGUE AND DEPARTMENT EXPECTATIONS RELATING TO PASTORAL SUPPORT

In this final section I have set out a non-exhaustive list of strategies to help you to navigate your pastoral role whilst avoiding taking on a disproportionate amount of the 'housekeeping work'.[10] I start by setting out some institutional level ideas and 'thinking points' before moving on to departmental level approaches and then, my main focus, personal strategies. It is not possible to be overly prescriptive here, due to the multitude of practice and procedures in place at different institutions, but it is hoped that these experience-based suggestions will contribute towards the development of student – and your – autonomy and resilience in relation to pastoral matters.

6.4.1 Create a Resource Bank of the Literature on Relevant Psychological Strategies and Sources of Help

Following a review of university websites, it is evident there is a lack of conformity in both the language and processes relating to pastoral support. This is true both when comparing institutions, and when comparing departments within the same institution. This may be something of a pandemic legacy, in that in recent years each institution has had to take a somewhat reactive approach to address a wealth of pastoral issues 'in the moment', meaning that their resources and practices have expanded and developed in a somewhat haphazard way. What could now be of assistance is a collective post pandemic 'reflective event' (which could also be a sector wide 'kinship event') whereby law schools work collaboratively to share these experiences so as to develop an open access suite of resources available to ECRs to help them to navigate this role. There could be materials founded on the literature on attachment theory and other relevant psychological strategies, together with information about local and national charitable organisations offering pastoral and psychological support. This would be of particular benefit for 'sidestep ECRs' who may not be enrolled in the teaching training courses that tend to be made available to 'home grown ECRs' and other colleagues who have entered academic life via the PhD route. It could also be made accessible by creating a resource bank based on realistic situations founded on experience, together with a series of suggested responses and next steps.

---

[10] See further Clare Mariskind, 'Teachers' care in higher education: contesting gendered constructions' (2014) 26(3) Gender and Education 306–20.

Within this resource bank there could be a set of specific resources to assist ECRs that give greater recognition to the ongoing issues with inappropriate sexual behaviour at universities and the 'lad culture' that sits behind it.[11] It is evident from discussions happening across the sector that there is problematic cultural practice taking place behind closed doors in shared accommodation and social spaces. This is aligned with the current well documented issues related to open access to pornography and misogynistic content on social media platforms. It is evident from my experience that when female students choose to speak out on this issue, it is often the maternal figures in their life to whom they turn, which in the law school tends to include the 'flown in ECRs' and 'sidestep ECRs' involved in tutorial teaching. I see this as an opportunity for there to be a collective 'reflective event' within the university sector, whereby we unite to acknowledge the extent of the issue and work together to support female students to navigate – and change – the cultural environment.

It is appreciated that in the short term it may not be possible for such a resource bank to be created at the sector level so a collation of materials on university or department staff websites is a more realistic objective, and one that will be encouraged as a consequence of writing this chapter.

6.4.2 Create a Formal Mentorship Structure

Following on from the above, I would suggest more could be done within individual departments or universities, and indeed the wider university sector, to provide formal mentorship structures to assist ECRs with the challenges associated with the pastoral support aspect of their role. This responds to the findings of the literature review by Westonby et al,[12] which found (amongst other things) that informal networks of support tend to be harder to access for women in academia, in part because there are too few female academics in senior positions. It is posited that if pastoral mentorship and support was more widely regarded as of significant value within the sector, it would perhaps become better recognised as part of the workload model, meaning that it would be possible for the most appropriate people to provide ECRs with more guidance and support. It seems to be that in our post COVID-19 environment an increasing number of people working within the University sector are recognising the important role played by pastoral supervisors, so I would encourage

---

[11] Cf. Carolyn Jackson and Vanita Sundaram, '"I have a sense that it's probably quite bad ...but because I don't see it, I don't know": staff perspectives on "lad culture" in higher education' (2021) 33(4) Gender and Education 435.

[12] Westoby, Dyson, Cowdell and Buescher (n 2).

you to engage with opportunities provided by your institutions for training and support.

6.4.3 Develop Techniques for Anticipation and Deflection

For the most part, the sector wide changes suggested above are beyond your control, so the rest of this chapter focuses on the more immediate techniques to consider, including anticipation and deflection of conversations relating to pastoral support.

It is suggested that one way for you to address the challenges of being asked for ad hoc pastoral support at the end of a class is to pre-empt it. For example, when teaching using resources that cover contentious and challenging material such that it requires content warnings, part of the messaging at the beginning of the session can be about reminding students to take advantage of the opportunities to access appropriate welfare support from central university services or dedicated departmental pastoral staff. Reminding students about the need to support each other within tutorial and friendship groups can also be useful.

Another approach is to anticipate the need for ad hoc end of lesson chats and accommodate them, such as by finishing the session a few minutes early to allow such conversations to take place, whilst ensuring that they fall outside break periods. This is not a long-term strategy – and it would not be appropriate to run short in teaching sessions as a matter of course – but it can be useful when 'reading the room' identifies that specific students may have immediate pastoral needs.

A final suggestion for deflection is around the need to promote visual messaging within the teaching environment. I would encourage you to suggest to your departments that information around pastoral support should be displayed with prominence in teaching and social spaces on campus. Signposting and promoting central university and student union activities and events can also help to reduce the volume of informal pastoral support.

6.4.4 Create an Evidence Trail of the Pastoral Work Undertaken

Most institutions have a workload model that attributes set times for pastoral roles. In my experience these have never been an accurate reflection of the actual time taken, as contributing factors vary year on year – even before the deluge of pastoral work that arose as a consequence of the COVID-19 pandemic (which is another factor that has led to inequity in the performance of pastoral roles).[13]

However, in instances where this role is taking up a disproportionate amount of time, it is useful for departmental managers to have evidence of this to ensure it is taken into account in work allocation in subsequent years.

Women in the law school are strongly encouraged to flag the impact of the 'housekeeping work/glory work' distinction, such as when departmental roles are being allocated. For example, having responsibility for a year group or a programme may bring kudos, but it can also bring an unexpectedly high administrative workload that needs to be appropriately recognised. I would encourage you, particularly if you're female, to push back on some aspects of these types of roles. To assist with these conversations, it is suggested you keep a record of specific examples of when an end of lesson chat, an inappropriate comment in class, an emergency situation or, a conversation linked to a uniting characteristic has led to a disproportionate amount of additional work. Such evidence would be of benefit to help to track the workload implications of the gendered nature of pastoral support, but it could also contribute to a greater collective understanding of the extent of the informal pastoral work undertaken within the sector. If sufficient time is available, I would also encourage you to seek out allies and share practice around your experiences of pastoral support so as to co-create a resource bank – and indeed an anecdote bank – when there is seen to be a need to approach management teams about the workload implications of providing effective care for students in a proportionate way.

6.4.5 Acknowledge and Accept that it is Part of the Role

There is a sentiment within the sector that as we are not mental health professionals the seemingly relentless demand for extra pastoral support should be met by default with deflection approaches, such as immediate signposting to specialised services within the wider university. I accept this in principle but would struggle to accept it in practice the next time a student seeks me out and then immediately starts to cry. Instead, I think we need to acknowledge and accept that pastoral support is part of our role, and work together to create structures and processes to ensure that this is provided in as equitable way as possible. In our post-pandemic world this can include greater acknowledgement that student mental health is a significant issue within the sector, which

---

[13] Jennifer Rode, Eileen Kennedy and Allison Littlejohn, 'Gender and the lived body experience of academic work during COVID-19' (2022) 47(1) Learning, Media and Technology 109–24.

needs greater recognition and support, such as with the creation of dedicated wellbeing advisors to work alongside, rather than replacing, the important pastoral responsibilities of ECRs.[14] Although a rather dramatic option, flagging recent news events and data collection that illustrate the damaging effect of failings in pastoral support could act as a catalyst for these types of conversations.[15] For me, writing this chapter has been an example of a 'reflective event', from which I will continue to strive to support colleagues and students in developing practices and resources to assist with pastoral support, autonomy and resilience.

6.5 SUMMARY

Navigating the pastoral role for ECRs is always challenging, and the purpose of this chapter is to share practice based on my experience as a woman, a parent and a former 'sidestep ECR'. Suggested action points for you to consider include the following:

1. Join or create a community of support with other ECRs so as to share practice around time efficient pastoral support, including suggested approaches to dealing with the 'trigger events' linked to curriculum content and classroom discussions.
2. Acknowledge the influence of uniting characteristics (including disability, ethnicity, sexuality, gender, life event) on your attitude towards pastoral support and the 'kinship events' you share with students and colleagues that you may (or may not) choose to engage with.
3. Familiarise yourself with the pastoral support resource available to you at the department, university and/or sector level, and use these alongside the 'reflective events' you experience to deepen your knowledge.
4. Where pastoral workloads start to feel unreasonable – especially where you feel your sex, gender or other personal characteristic is influencing the expectations of colleagues and/or students about your role – collate information and evidence about this so as to draw it to the attention of your departmental management team.

---

[14] For more on this in the context of a different disciplinary area in the UK see Deesha Chadha, Andreas Kogelbauer, James Campbell, Klaus Hellgardt, Marsha Maraj, Umang Shah, Clemens Brechtelsbauer and Colin Hale, 'Are the kids alright? Exploring students' experiences of support mechanisms to enhance wellbeing on an engineering programme in the UK' (2021) 46(5) European Journal of Engineering Education 662–77.

[15] See further at: officeforstudents.org.uk/advice-and-guidance/promoting-equal-opportunities/effective-practice/suicide-prevention/ (accessed 2 October 2023).

7. How to offer effective pastoral support in a distance learning institution

Liz Hardie, Francine Ryan

7.1 INTRODUCTION

The Open University (OU) is the UK's largest university offering flexible online distance education. The online learning market has shown significant growth in recent years and there are increasing numbers of universities now offering online courses or traditional learning delivery in hybrid or digital formats. The focus of this chapter is to help you understand better how to support students to thrive online.

Students at the OU combine study with work and caring responsibilities meaning that pastoral support must be designed and delivered flexibly to respond to meet the needs of a diverse body of students. In this chapter we share our experiences of supporting students online. We discuss what pastoral support means and explore different ways of offering such support, drawing on a range of case studies from the OU. We share an institutional framework of student support and projects designed by the law school to target particular groups of students that may be useful for adoption by academics at other institutions. The online environment presents challenges for supporting students and careful consideration needs to be given to how to overcome those barriers.

The OU model of personal support is provided by our tutors (also known as Associate Lecturers). We recognise that different institutions have different modes of support for their students therefore when we refer to tutors, we are including all academic staff who might provide pastoral support. We share our tips for good practice and explore how you can use regular communication and encouragement to support and personalise the learning experience of online students.[1] First, we explore how the OU teaches and provides support

---

[1] See Chapter 9 to contrast some of the issues raised in supporting students in a face-to-face setting and reflect how they are different/similar to those in an online environment.

7.2 DISTANCE LEARNING AT THE OPEN UNIVERSITY

The OU was founded in 1969 and has a reputation as a world leader in supported distance learning with a mission to make higher education accessible to all. It is a four-nation university with a presence in Wales, Ireland, Scotland, and England. Most of our undergraduate curriculum has no pre-entry requirements meaning that we are open to all. This means that students can study with us with no or very few formal educational qualifications. There is no such thing as a 'typical' OU student. We have students from all walks of life, all ages and at different stages of their lives. We also have the largest number of disabled students compared with any other university in UK and Europe.[2] There are a range of motivations for study: for some students it is for a change of career or to improve their work prospects, for others it is for personal growth. Most of our students are working either part or full time and have caring responsibilities: when thinking about pastoral support you must be aware of how time poor distance students are.

Our students are not required to physically attend university at a designated time or place. Instead, we offer 'supported online learning' that allows students to study from any location flexibly around their work and caring commitments. Instead of attending lectures and seminars students study online at their own pace with all the learning materials provided through our virtual learning environment (VLE). Each module has a week-by-week study planner which links to the work that the student needs to complete.

The model for the delivery of the learning materials is often different in a distance learning setting. An academic will provide support via email, telephone, online conferencing platforms and forums where they offer guidance and support on the module materials. The provision of detailed feedback on students' assignments is at the heart of OU teaching. Academics are required to give written and prescribed feedback to students to support them in their learning.

7.3 WHAT IS PASTORAL SUPPORT?

There are many definitions of pastoral support within the higher education context. Pastoral support is often distinguished from academic support, com-

---

[2] See also Chapter 11.

monly called teaching or tuition, which is aimed at developing a students' knowledge and understanding or cognitive skills.[3] Non-academic or pastoral support focuses on developing and supporting the student's ability to participate in learning and succeed in their studies and is something you may be required to do either as part of a role such as a personal tutor, or informally during your contact with students. Pastoral support often involves issues around student wellbeing such as managing the emotional and social impact of study or encouraging students to stay motivated. It may also involve supporting students with their time management, prioritisation and organisational skills.[4]

In face-to-face institutions where students and tutors meet regularly in lectures, seminars and during office hours, pastoral support is often provided by either course tutors or nominated pastoral tutors. Rapport and trust between students and academics can more easily be developed face to face, where you are having spontaneous conversations which use visual cues and body language to support the conversation. However, in an online or distance learning environment, you may find that opportunities to offer pastoral support do not arise so naturally and so you will need to intentionally consider ways of offering this support and think about how you might build in these opportunities into your teaching. Pastoral support is also often provided by different teams within the university, so you should ensure you know the various ways in which your faculty or university offers pastoral support to students and how to refer students to other services.

We will now focus on four case studies which demonstrate different ways of providing pastoral support to students in a distance learning environment.

7.4 WORKING IN TEAMS

At the OU the Student Support team combines groups of staff from the Faculty and Academic services to support students through their university journey. In this section we consider how you might work in partnership with those teams to support your students.

---

[3] See also Chapters 4 and 6.
[4] Angeles Sánchez-Elvira Paniagua and Ormond Simpson, 'Developing Student Support for Open and Distance Learning: The EMPOWER Project' (2018) 1 Journal of Interactive Media in Education 9, 5.

7.4.1 Student Support

The OU provides subject specific Student Support teams (SST) to support students through their study journey.[5] Academics can refer students to the SST, and they will contact the student to offer further support. It is important for an academic to work in partnership with the SST and to know when to refer students. You need to be familiar with the policy of your institution, but in an online setting it is important that an academic closely monitors student engagement because students can more easily 'disappear' from their studies.

The signs you should be aware of that may indicate a student is struggling are:

1. Lack of engagement with the VLE.
2. Failure to respond to emails.
3. Sending lots of emails that suggest a student is not confident with the learning materials.
4. Failure to submit an assignment.

If you become aware a student is having difficulties in the first instance, contact the student via email or telephone to explore the issues impacting on their studies. They may need to reduce their study intensity, or they may be experiencing a short-term issue that is causing them difficulties that you can suggest practical solutions to.

Within the SST team there are also specialist Educational Advisors who provide educational support and guidance for students in more complex cases to enable them to make appropriate study choices. Personal Learning Advisors work in partnership with tutors to offer mentoring and coaching support to students from traditionally disadvantaged and marginalised groups.[6] They offer tailored and personalised support to those students who face complex problems that might impact on their ability to engage and complete their studies. Your institution may have similar specialist teams to which you can refer students facing more complex challenges.

7.4.2 Tutors

The relationship between tutors and students is critical to ensuring that students are supported in their learning journey. The tutor at the OU has two main

---

[5] Chapter 5 explores the role of Student Support Officers at the University of Leeds; you may want to contrast the different mechanisms for proving support to students.

[6] See also Chapters 3, 6, 8, 9, 10 and 11.

functions: the first is to mark assessments and provide personalised feedback to help students to develop and learn. The second is to facilitate the students' learning by guiding and supporting them. The tutor is the first point of contact for a student and are often described as the 'face' of the OU. This may be different from your experiences at other institutions where course lecturers have a direct relationship with students.

The development of relationships can be more challenging in an online learning environment meaning that students might be more reluctant to ask for help. It is important to develop personal connections with students because it is very unlikely an academic will meet them in person. Although the role of the tutor is to provide academic support, pastoral issues often impact upon the student's ability to make progress on their module, therefore there is a strong correlation between the academic and pastoral support a tutor provides. For example, students might request extensions for submission of their assignments because of circumstances impacting on their ability to study. Students might have events in their lives that mean they cannot continue to study at this time, and tutors will work closely with the SST to navigate their learning journey.

7.5 PEER MENTORING

Many universities provide mentoring to students in their first year.[7] The OU introduced peer mentoring for our new law students in 2020 to explore whether this could be provided in an online environment. Peer mentoring is where a more experienced student provides guidance and support to a new student, and this complements the work of the tutor.[8] Studies from face-to-face institutions show that peer mentoring can improve student retention, progression and attainment as well as addressing student wellbeing and promoting peer communities of practice.[9] We therefore introduced a small peer mentoring pilot for 50 new students studying their first law module in 2019–20 and expanded it to all new students starting law in October 2020 (2,500 students in total).

In order to introduce this scheme, we had to obtain agreement and funding from the faculty and university. We found it was better to start by proposing a small pilot project which will be evaluated, as it is often easier to persuade

---

[7] See also Chapter 6.
[8] Carol Edwards, Lorraine Gregory and Liz Hardie, 'Setting up a Pilot Peer Mentoring Programme in the Online Environment' (2021) 2 Journal of Rights and Justice 8.
[9] Ralph Hall and Zarni Jaugietis, 'Developing Peer Mentoring through Evaluation' (2011) 36 Innov High Educ 41–52, DOI 10.1007/s10755-010-9156-6.

key stakeholders to support and fund such a project (particularly with reference to the aforementioned benefits of such projects).[10]

Peer mentoring has different models including 1-2-1, one to many and many to many approaches. As one of our aims was to reduce student isolation by encouraging peer support, we decided initially to use a one-to-many approach where one mentor supported a small group of around five to eight students. Following feedback from students and mentors after the first pilot we changed our approach for the second larger scale pilot, and this was organised on a many-to-many approach. We divided our students into four geographic areas, each of which was supported by a group of four mentors working together. We recruited our mentors by an expression of interest with a criterion that they had to have studied the first law module within the last two years, and we received more applications than available spaces. No incentive was offered to the mentors to take part, although they did receive training at the start of the project and a certificate at the end detailing the skills they had developed and used during the project.

The mentoring took place through forums where students asynchronously posted messages and discussed pastoral issues. Academic queries were directed to the academic tutors. The mentors also provided some online synchronous sessions which were a mixture of informal online coffee events (timed to occur at critical times during the module such as before the first tutorial or assessment), and student led sessions targeted at different students (such as those studying with English as a second language or with a disability). The programme of events was designed by the mentors themselves using a co-creation approach, drawing upon the mentors' experience as students.

If you are thinking of introducing online peer mentoring, you will need to consider safeguarding, confidentiality and ensuring appropriate student behaviour online. We provided the mentors with a dedicated tutor to support them and to monitor the forums to ensure appropriate behaviour online. We also hosted the forums and meetings on the university VLE so there was no need for mentors and mentees to exchange private contact details. As far as we are aware students used the VLE and did not exchange contact details. We ran a training day for the mentors which covered safeguarding, online boundaries

---

[10] See e.g. Jane Andrews and Robin Clark, 'Peer mentoring works!', available at: publications.aston.ac.uk/id/eprint/17968/ (accessed 2 October 2023) 21; Emma Jones, 'Connectivity, socialization and identity formation. Exploring mental well-being in online distance learning law students' in Rachael Field and Caroline Strevens (eds), *Educating for Well-Being in Law: Positive Professional Identities and Practice* (Routledge, 2020) 103–16; Jennifer Finlay-Jones and Nicola Ross, 'Peer Mentoring for Law Students – Improving the First Year Advocacy Experience' (2006) 40 Law Teacher 23, 39.

and how to use the online forums and host online sessions. We designed and ran this training day ourselves as there was no generic university training available. However, there are people within the university with expertise who may run individual sessions, so do identify others within your university able to help with training. For example, one of our educational advisers ran the session on safeguarding, or your university safeguarding team may offer to help with this. Some of our tutors who regularly use online forums and online sessions with students ran the practical training sessions, while academics who moderate large online forums offered to lead a discussion about online boundaries.

Peer mentoring offers students many benefits and we would encourage you to consider whether and how it might be used within your institution. From the mentee's perspective it can improve confidence, offer an opportunity to ask 'silly questions' they are reluctant to approach academics about, and encourage a sense of belonging to an academic community which occurs more naturally in a face-to-face environment. From the mentors' perspective, they form strong communities with their fellow mentors; one mentor commented that the friendships built amongst the mentors had been 'the best part of the project'. They also developed valuable employability skills and improved their own learning by reflecting more deeply on their past studies and skills development.

You should be aware that developing a peer mentoring scheme does require time to plan the project so that it meets the institutions' requirements, as well as selecting and training the mentors and arranging relevant IT access for participants. However, once the scheme was set up, the mentors' enthusiasm and energy meant the project required little further intervention and it provided valuable peer pastoral support for students. If you are considering setting up a peer mentoring scheme, you will need to think about the following:

- Obtaining faculty and university support and funding.
- Deciding on the mentoring model: individual or group mentoring, which students or courses, how the project will run and which IT platforms.
- Liaising with your IT support services to ensure the scheme is set up and access is given to the relevant members of staff and students.
- Addressing confidentiality and data protection issues.
- Recruiting suitable mentors.
- Training mentors, including safeguarding.
- Recruiting mentees and matching them to the mentors.
- Allocating academic time to support the mentors during the programme.

7.6 USING FORUMS

The Open University has used asynchronous online forums to provide academic student support for many years. Students and tutors have access to an online forum where information, messages and questions can be posted which remain visible and available to participants throughout the duration of the course. Typically, the tutor will moderate the forum and start new discussion threads every couple of weeks. This may include posting links to news articles or online resources, posing a question for students to prompt discussion, posting information from the module team, or reminding students of forthcoming assessments, tutorials, or other study activities. This enables information to be shared, or a discussion to take place, between students and the tutor asynchronously at a time to suit the participants. In 2020–21 we decided to use the forums to provide pastoral support to targeted students; students studying at full time intensity; and students aged 18–21 years. Alongside synchronous online sessions, both these projects offered support through dedicated forums managed and moderated by tutors. The full-time intensity project had three tutors providing support, one for each year of study (first year, second year and third years), while the younger students project had two tutors working together to support students. Threads posted on the forums included icebreaker activities, information and signposting to relevant resources, discussions about general legal topics, Q&As with more experienced students offering study tips, general study skills information and threads relating to wellbeing and motivation.

Linking posts about general legal topics to topical issues can be a good way of engaging students or prompting student reflections. For example:

- Icebreakers asking students to post their favourite law or legal themes book, film or TV series are always popular – and generate suggestions for future reading or watching! This can be linked to questions about the extent to which those books, films or TV series accurately reflect the law or practice of law.
- Posting a news article and asking for student comments can work well, particularly where it is an interesting or high-profile issue or involves a well-known celebrity.
- Using contemporary events to prompt a discussion can also lead to interesting discussions.

Having set up forums to offer pastoral support to students, we discovered that overall active participation on these forums was limited. For example, the younger students' forum had 18 threads of which 12 threads involved only the tutors' posting messages. However, even if a forum appears to be little used by students, it is common that most learners either subscribe to or read posts on the forum as 'read only participants,' lurking on the forums to absorb information even if not contributing posts themselves.[11] The biggest thread was the welcome and introductions thread; eight students posted messages on the thread but 125 students read the thread, with a further 14 subscribing to the forum and receiving the message via email. Even a thread about wellbeing posted by the tutor with no active student responses had 40 student readers and 14 subscribers. The tutors involved in these projects became frustrated and demoralised by the lack of interaction with students and we had to remind them that a lack of response by students does not necessarily indicate the support is not having any effect; there will be students reading and absorbing the information provided, even if not actively participating.

We also became aware that many students were not aware of these forums, even though we had sent out an email to students at the start of the academic year to advertise them. The sheer volume of emails sent to students at the start of the academic year meant it had not been read or remembered by students. When setting up online support schemes, you therefore need to also have a robust communication strategy; it is often better to inform students on multiple occasions and by different methods. You need to ensure students offered support through these asynchronous methods are aware of their availability, know how to access it, and understand its purpose. This is particularly important for distance learning students who are often time poor, as they are managing studies alongside other commitments.

Finally, some students and tutors expressed a preference for social media platforms as a means of providing asynchronous support, instead of forums hosted on the university VLE. This raised some interesting questions about perceived formal and informal learning spaces, the importance of easy access to platforms (with forums requiring a sign-in to the university VLE), whether and how to moderate platforms providing pastoral support, and how to ensure confidentiality and safeguarding on a third-party platform. Our institution had reservations about using social media platforms due to the concerns that this requires the sharing of student contact information (emails or telephone numbers) with other students and the accessibility of such technology. The use of social media can exclude students in digital poverty who may not have access to a smart phone or internet, or students with a disability who cannot use the platform. Your institution may have a policy about the use of social media

---

[11] Janine Delahunty, '"Who am I?": Exploring identity in online discussion forums' (2012) 53 International Journal of Educational Research 417; Susi Peacock and John Cowan, 'Promoting sense of belonging in online learning communities of inquiry at accredited courses' (2019) 23(2) Online Learning 67–81.

to support students, so it is important to discuss with them the possible use of third-party platforms.

7.7 CHALLENGES

Providing pastoral support to students online has several challenges, and we will now discuss some issues which can hinder attempts to provide online support.

First, when studying online it is much harder to develop a sense of belonging to a community between students and tutor, or between students and students; online and distance learner students report concerns about isolation and negative impacts on their wellbeing.[12] Interactions which occur naturally in a lecture theatre with tutors, or at the end of a seminar between students, do not happen in online spaces. Some students who may have contributed in a face-to-face setting find posting on an online forum or taking part in online group work daunting or threatening.[13] This may be due to a lack of confidence, or concerns about misunderstandings due to the lack of visual cues and difficulties discerning the meaning behind others' communications. The permanency of the communication (for example on a forum, or in online sessions which are recorded) may also deter students.[14]

There are ways of encouraging a sense of community online, but you will need to deliberately design and nurture these. You can make sure you are the first to post on an online forum or speak in an online room, adopt a welcoming and friendly tone, acknowledge students' contributions positively and encourage students to talk to each other and not just to you. These will all help to build community. Designing activities, including icebreakers, to be inclusive is also important.[15] For example, asking students about a book, TV or movie which relates to the subject being studied is something which is accessible and can usually be answered by everyone. If you facilitate discussion and build a sense of community, it will be more likely that students approach you or a fellow student for support.

Secondly, when providing pastoral support online you need to decide whether the support should be provided synchronously or asynchronously. Synchronous support by telephone, online meeting or webchat is more immediate and gives the opportunity to ask questions and deal with any ambiguity

---

[12] Delahunty (n 11) 407–20.
[13] Peacock and Cowan (n 11).
[14] Delahunty (n 11) 416.
[15] Krystle Phirangee and Alesia Malec, 'Othering in online learning: an examination of social presence, identity, and sense of community' (2017) 38(2) Distance Education 160–72.

or misunderstandings. However, it can be difficult to arrange a mutually convenient time for such a meeting, particularly if the student is working, has caring responsibilities or is in a different time zone. There is also no record of these discussions; some platforms do allow for recordings to be made but asking for consent to record the conversation may inhibit students. Asynchronous methods such as email, forums, some social media platforms, and text are more flexible in that students can participate at a time and place to suit them. In theory, therefore, they are more accessible methods of communication available to a greater number of students. Where support is provided to a group, responses to one student's query benefit the other students who may have similar questions. It can also improve students' confidence as they realise that others also have questions or are struggling with aspects of their study.[16] However, some students will not feel comfortable raising concerns or questions in a group setting, and some students do not participate in group discussions due to concerns about confidentiality. There is also a greater risk of misunderstanding with asynchronous methods of communication, and the delays inherent in this method of communication may also be detrimental if the concerns are time sensitive. You should therefore set expectations for response times with any asynchronous method of support.

Both synchronous and asynchronous methods rely on students being proactive in contacting you when they need support and asking for help. We know however that some students will find it difficult to do this and the third challenge of providing pastoral support online is the greater risk of students 'falling between the cracks' in an online environment. You may find it easier in a face-to-face environment to identify students who miss lectures, appear distressed or behave atypically. Where students are studying independently at a distance, it is much more difficult to identify struggling students to proactively provide support. There are some ways, however, of identifying students who need pastoral support.

The first and most important thing you can do is to establish a friendly, welcoming environment so students not only know how to contact you for support, but also feel confident in doing so. We have found that students will often make contact initially with a minor or general issue (I don't understand X, or I am struggling with Y) and when they receive a prompt and sympathetic response, they will then disclose the issue which is actually causing them concern.

---

[16] Ella Kahu, 'Increasing the emotional engagement of first year mature-aged distance students: Interest and belonging' (2014) 5(2) The International Journal of the First Year in Higher Education 45–55.

It is also important to build into your tutoring activities specific times to contact students to check on their progress. An individual approach encourages a response if there are problems, and so email or telephone is a good way of doing this. You can target this contact at important stages of the course (such as around assessment submissions), or times when you know students may drop out (such as shortly after the course starts or when a difficult concept is being taught). If timed correctly, this proactive contact will allow you to provide support and interventions to get students back on track before they drop out. It has been described as 'one of the key activities of a tutor in ODL [online distance learning], far more so perhaps than in conventional education.'[17]

Your institution may provide learning analytics which allow you to monitor student progress, so you can identify and contact students who have fallen behind in their studies to offer support. At the OU we can see when a student last logged onto the module website and how many times they logged on in the last week. This allows us to identify when students either stop looking at the module website, or when their behaviour changes so they are online less frequently. However, it is wise to be cautious in how you approach students and not make assumptions, as sometimes students' studying habits can change because of pre-planned work or family commitments, or they may have downloaded materials and are not studying online. Your institution may have other forms of student monitoring or learning analytics which can be used to identify students who are potentially struggling.[18]

Finally, the last challenge in providing pastoral support online is supporting students in digital poverty who have no (or limited) access to the internet. 10 million people in the UK lack basic digital skills.[19] This includes students who lack access to the internet completely (1.5 million households in 2021), those with slow or unreliable internet or concerns about broadband cost, those who lack an appropriate device, those who lack the digital skills necessary for online study, and those who cannot access materials online due to a disability.

---

[17] Ormond Simpson, *Supporting Students in Online, Open and Distance Learning* (2nd edn, Routledge, 2018) 46.

[18] For more information on learning analytics see Dragan Gasevic, Yi-Shan Tsai, Shane Dawson and Abelardo Pardo, 'How do we start? An approach to learning analytics adoption in higher education' (2019) 36(4) The International Journal of Information and Learning Technology 342–53; Billy Tak-Ming Wong, 'The Benefits of Learning Analytics in Open and Distance Education: A Review of the Evidence' in Myint Swe Khine, *Emerging Trends in Learning Analytics: Leveraging the Power of Education Data* (Brill ProQuest eBook Central, 2019), available at: researchgate.net/publication/330555393_Emerging_Trends_in_Learning_Analytics_Leveraging_the_Power_of_Education_Data (accessed 2 October 2023).

[19] Good Things Foundation, 'The Digital Divide' (Good Things Foundation, 2021), available at: goodthingsfoundation.org/the-digital-divide/ (accessed 2 October 2023).

The Office for Students reported in 2021 that during the COVID-19 lockdown, 52% of students said their learning was impacted by slow or unreliable internet connection, with 8% 'severely' affected.[20] Supporting students online can be challenging in these circumstances.

You cannot therefore assume that all students will have ready access to the internet or a device they can use to study. Asking students the best way to contact them can help bridge this digital divide. We have noted an increasing number of students who access the internet and study via a smart mobile phone, and they sometimes prefer text contact rather than email (as the latter requires internet access and incurs cost). However, you will need to check your institution's policy around the use of personal telephone numbers as texting or calling from a personal mobile may be prohibited. If this is the case, it is possible to text using an alternative number through an online web-based provider, although again you should check your institution's policy on this.

As students may have difficulties accessing materials online, you should ensure any student resources can be downloaded and read off-line. This reduces internet costs and mitigates against unreliable or slow internet connection. You may also be able to signpost students to any institutional scholarships or bursaries covering the cost of technological devices or internet costs. Where you support students who cannot access the internet at all, you will need to agree with them the best way of contacting them and how you will send any necessary information to them. Your institution may be able to assist with this as they are likely to have a process in place to support students who require printed materials due to a disability.

7.8 CONCLUSION

This chapter has considered some of the ways pastoral support can be provided online, some of the challenges this presents and advice on how to respond to the issues we can face. The emphasis is on creating a personal relationship with the students where they feel confident in approaching you for support. Institutions will also have valuable resources and expertise to complement your work. From our experience a holistic approach to pastoral support is required that provides a clear pathway to support students through their learning journey.

---

[20] Office for Students 'Digital Poverty Risks Leaving Students Behind' (Good Things Foundation 2020) goodthingsfoundation.org/the-digital-divide/ accessed 29 April 2022

7.9 SUMMARY

1. Make sure you provide a welcoming, inclusive environment so students feel comfortable contacting you for support.
2. Proactively check in with your students as to their progress, including using any learning analytics available to you, so that students do not struggle unnoticed.
3. Consider whether individual or group support provided synchronously or asynchronously is most appropriate.
4. Think about whether the relevant pastoral support is best provided by you, fellow students, or the university student support teams.
5. Where support is provided online, check students have the means and skills to access that support.
6. Ensure students know when you are available for pastoral support and when they can expect a response.
7. Think about what kind of training or advice you might need to provide effective online pastoral support.
8. When you are offering support, reflect on how you can try to develop a personal relationship with the student and boost the student's confidence.
9. Remember it is often harder to pick up non-verbal clues and communication can more easily be misunderstood online, so consider carefully how you frame your interactions with students.
10. In online environments it is critical to consider how pastoral support can be interwoven into the overall teaching and learning strategy.

8. You see me, but can you hear me? Let's talk about race
Iwi Ugiagbe-Green

Talking about race can be challenging. It is the fear that creates the challenge. The fear of getting the terminology wrong. The fear of expressing an opinion that is deemed racist. The fear of the discomfort that comes with unlearning. The fear of not knowing how to respond to questions about race. So rather than face fear, it becomes the elephant in the room.

But fear is an insufficient reason to not bring important conversations of race and learning of law. Underlying principles of law are about protecting rights and liberties and fairness. As an educator of law, particularly if you are an early career educator, it is really difficult but important to work through your fear to uphold these principles.

A widely held belief is that in being 'colourblind' in our praxis, we are being universally fair to everyone. This is simply not true: if you do not talk about race, you do not acknowledge difference and diversity. You do not develop the language and literacy of race and you ignore the realities of systemic racism. To work towards addressing issues of systemic racism, we must foster inclusive learning communities and employ anti-racist pedagogy in our praxis. Kishimoto provides a comprehensive explanation of anti-racist pedagogy:

> Anti-racist pedagogy is not about simply incorporating racial content into courses, curriculum, and discipline. It is also about how one teaches, even in courses where race is not the subject matter. It begins with the faculty's awareness and self-reflection of their social position and leads to application of this analysis in their teaching, but also in their discipline, research, and departmental, university, and community work. In other words, anti-racist pedagogy is an organizing effort for institutional and social change that is much broader than teaching in the classroom.[1]

An important question posed by this chapter is 'Whose rights and liberties are being protected in the classroom, in how we teach law, if we do not talk

---

[1] Kyoko Kishimoto, 'Anti-racist pedagogy: from faculty's self-reflection to organizing within and beyond the classroom' (2018) 21(4) Race Ethnicity and Education 540–54, DOI: 10.1080/13613324.2016.1248824, p.540.

about race?' It is a critical issue of race equity, particularly to students who are racialised as non-white (so called, 'BAME'; Black, Asian and Minority ethnic or 'BME'; Black and minority ethnic). However, by not talking about the importance and significance of the social construction of race and its impact on law making, the rule of law and its application in a societal context, everyone misses out on socially relevant education excellence.

The category of 'white' is not a category of ethnicity, but a category of race. However, 'BAME' and 'BME' are terms of ethnicity, used as the language of the higher education sector to make comparisons between white and non-white individuals. And as such, ethnicity is used as a proxy for race. Issues regarding racial literacy and the complexities of sub-groups within all homogeneous groupings of racialised categories (including white), are important in the context of better understanding the nuances of experience across different racialised groups. However, these issues are beyond the scope of discussion in this book chapter.

In this chapter, I am using 'BAME' and 'BME' when citing reports and data sources relating to law education. In instances where I provide my own analysis of differences between students racialised as white and students racialised as non-white, I will use the expression, 'racially minoritised.' This term acknowledges that whilst non-white people make up the global majority, it is non-white people who are homogenised into categories of BAME and BME for analysis and therefore, minoritised.[2]

8.1 LET'S TALK ABOUT RACE

Conversations about race are important, because without them the existence of racism and its impact cannot be acknowledged or addressed. Without race, racism does not exist. American lawyer, professor, and civil rights activist, Professor Derrick Bell, explains, 'the reality is that we live in a society in which racism has been internalized and institutionalized.'[3] It is a society that produced a culture from whose inception racial discrimination has been a regulating force.

Inequitable outcomes for racially minoritised people begin from the moment they are born e.g. a Black woman is four times more likely to die during child-

---

[2] Line Predelli, Beatrice Halsaa, Cecile Thun and Adriana Sandu, *Majority-minority relations in contemporary women's movements: strategic sisterhood* (Palgrave Macmillan, 2012).

[3] Derrick Bell, 'Racism is here to stay: now what' (1991) 35(1) Howard Law Journal 79–94.

birth than a white woman.[4] These inequalities continue through to the school system e.g. exclusion rates for Black Caribbean students in English schools are up to six times higher than those of their white peers in some local authorities.[5] And then to university, a Black student with AAA at A Level compared with a white student with BBC at A level is less likely to get a 'good degree' (a 2:1 or 1:1 degree classification award).[6] These persistent and pervasive gaps have a sustained impact on inter-generational wealth, access to capital, access to healthcare provision and so on. These inequitable outcomes are the consequence of discriminatory impacts of social systems disproportionately affecting people who are not racialised as white.[7]

As educators, we all have a responsibility to work towards protecting the rights and liberties of all our students, not just those who are centred as normative by society. We must also protect and support the marginalised and minoritised. Engaging in conversations about race in our spaces of engagement, though perhaps fear inducing for some, can also be liberating for everyone.

Freedom and liberation are gained from the courage in feeling the fear but not allowing the fear to conquer action toward liberation. Additionally, the fear of the permanence of racism is not sufficient reason to not engage in anti-racism work.

8.2 LAW EDUCATION IN ENGLAND AND WALES

The solicitors' profession in England and Wales (E&W) has undoubtedly changed in terms of its composition and size over the last 30 years or so. In the case of ethnicity, there has been an acceleration of new admissions by Black, Asian and minority ethnic ('BAME') solicitors over the last ten years. The Solicitors' Regulation Authority (SRA) reports there has been an increase in the proportion of Black, Asian and minority ethnic ('BAME') lawyers working in law firms (now one in five). This is up 7%, from 14% in 2014 to 21% in 2017. In 2015, 11% of the UK workforce were BAME. This increase is largely due to the rise in Asian lawyers in the profession, up from 9% in 2014 to 14%

---

[4] MBRRACE-UK, *Saving Lives, Improving Mothers' Care Report* (National Perinatal Epidemiology Unit (NPEU), University of Oxford, 2021).

[5] Jessica Perera, *How Black working-class youth are excluded and criminalised in the English school system. A London case study* (Institute of Race Relations Report, 2020).

[6] Universities UK National Union of Students, *Black Asian and Minority Ethnic Student Attainment at UK Universities: Closing the Gap* (2019).

[7] Omar Khan, *Economic inequality and racial inequalities in the UK: Current evidence and the possible effects of systemic economic change* Runnymede Trust (2019), available at: friendsprovidentfoundation.org/wp-content/uploads/2019/01/Runnymede-report.pdf (accessed 3 October 2023).

in 2017. Black lawyers make up 3%, which has risen by 1% since 2014 and now reflects those in employment in the UK (3%). The proportion of Asian lawyers in law firms is 14% compared to 6% of the UK workforce. Asian lawyers make up two thirds of all 'BAME' lawyers.

This trend also reflects an increase in the ethnic diversity of students studying law in Higher Education institutions. Higher Education Statistics Agency (HESA) 2019/20 data reports UK domiciled law undergraduate students of known ethnicity comprise of 66% white students (54,390), 9% Black students (7,285), 17% Asian students (14,085), 5% Mixed (4,300) and 3% Other (2,250).[8]

Of course, not all students who study law go on to become solicitors. However, what these increases in ethnic diversity in the solicitor's profession and Higher Education law programmes demonstrate is a shift in widening access to law and the increasing ethnic diversity of the student pipeline to the profession. Representation in the profession is very important: 'It's hard to be, what you can't see.'[9]

Although representation of racially diverse groups continues to increase, inequitable outcomes relating to non-white groups remain prevalent. The Law Society Gazette reports the success rate for white graduates with a 2.1 degree achieving pupillage (39.3%) is more than double that of BME candidates (18%). Among pupils with a first-class degree, 59.4% of white students obtained pupillage compared with 41.6% of BME candidates. It is not the case that BME students have less 'aptitude' or 'ability' for law.[10]

However, according to figures published by the Solicitors Regulation Authority, 66% of white students passed the Solicitors Qualifying Exam (SQE1), compared to 39%of Black students and 43% of Asian students.[11] These figures across different racialised groups mirror a national degree awarding gap between 'BAME' and white students in higher education in the UK, that is not predicted to close until 2070–71.[12]

---

[8] See hesa.ac.uk/news/09-02-2021/he-student-data-201920 (accessed 3 October 2023).

[9] See childrensdefense.org/child-watch-columns/health/2015/its-hard-to-be-what-you-cant-see/ (accessed 3 October 2023).

[10] Max Walters, 'White candidates twice as likely to achieve bar pupillage, bar regulator reveals' (2017), available at: lawgazette.co.uk/law/white-candidates-twice-as-likely-to-achieve-pupillage-bar-regulator-reveals/5064032.article (accessed 3 October 2023).

[11] Louis Goss, 'Law Society flags attainment gap between white and ethnic minority students' (2022), available at: cityam.com/law-society-flags-attainment-gap-between-white-and-ethnic-minority-students/ (accessed 3 October 2023).

[12] Natasha Codiroli-McMaster, 'Ethnicity awarding gaps in higher education' Advance HE (2021), available at: advance-he.ac.uk/knowledge-hub/ethnicity-awarding-gaps-uk-higher-education-201920 (accessed 3 October 2023).

Furthermore, racially diverse staff representation in law schools and in higher education institutions, remains an issue. Only 140 academic staff at professorial level identify as Black, equating to 0.7% out of more than 21,000 professors. Nearly 18,000 or 85% identify as white, 1,360 or 6% as Asian, and more than 2,000 or 9% as unidentified or from other ethnic backgrounds. The widening access and resultant enhanced diversity within the law professions means there is an enhanced need to foster inclusive learning environments and curricula embracing and including everyone. Inclusive learning environments lower barriers to learning and foster a sense of belonging across and within different intersecting groups.[13] Those who are excluded are 'othered,' experiencing exclusion on the basis of not fitting in within the norms of a social group. Racially minoritised people are hyper-visible by their skin colour and other immutable physical attributes. They are often othered, minoritised and marginalised by more dominant racialised groups. The impact of this is devastating and can lead to students withdrawing from their programme (for example, Black students are almost one and a half times more likely to drop out of university than white or Asian students).[14]

Inclusive spaces should not marginalise or minoritise. However, it is important to note that inclusive and anti-racist are not synonyms. All learning spaces should be inclusive, safe spaces of learning for all students. However, anti-racist learning approaches are intentional and purposeful in their actions to mitigate systemic racism. An anti-racist approach requires an examination of racism in different contexts, including the personal, interpersonal, institutional, and cultural. Adopting such an approach requires change to existing traditional ('colourblind') pedagogic praxis. Bramble and Bhadur explain the legal academy have been reluctant to alter traditional methods of teaching. They suggest tangible, empirical evidence obtained from data-driven cognitive learning science research demonstrates that active learning is integral to an effective anti-racist pedagogical approach. In this context, active learning is that which is not passive, but where the learner constructs knowledge through their sharing of and engagement in experiences in and outside of the classroom. Active learning not only improves learning outcomes for all students, but also mitigates the structural effects of racism in the classroom thereby increasing racial equity.[15]

---

[13] See also Chapters 2 and 4.
[14] Nigel Keohane and Katherine Petrie, 'On course for success? Student retention at university' London: Social Market Foundation (2017), available at: smf.co.uk/publications/course-success-student-retention-university/ (accessed 3 October 2023).
[15] Catherine Bramble and Rory D. Bahadur, 'Actively Achieving Greater Racial Equity in the Law School Classroom' (2022) Cleveland State Law Review, available at: dx.doi.org/10.2139/ssrn.4022267 (accessed 3 October 2023).

The need to adopt anti-racist approaches is clear, as is the responsibility of legal educators to advance social equality. Law should be taught in the social context in which it is applied. In practice, this means issues of discrimination & racism, within the context of social issues such as the global pandemic and associated health & education inequalities across different racialised groups, should not be preserved for jurisprudence or legal ethics, but discussed as part of an active learning approach to law in general.

8.3   A CASE STUDY FROM MY OWN (ACCOUNTING) PRACTICE

One area of overlap between my subject discipline (Accounting) and Law is taxation. The tax system is viewed as 'colourblind.' However, if we incorporate the social context of the personal tax system into teaching of personal tax we acknowledge, for example, that inter-generational wealth is a racialised issue.

Personal wealth and the benefits of wealth have accrued to different racialised groups inequitably. It is a fact that the wealth of Britain was in large part built on slave labour mobilised principally through transatlantic slave trade and colonial exploitation. However, if we turn to a contemporary example of how capitalism and economic wealth remains a racialised issue, the Windrush scandal is a case in point. Citizens from the Commonwealth arrived in the UK before British nationality and immigration law made any distinction between British subjects, whether born and living in the UK or elsewhere in the Empire (the existence of which has its roots in imperialism and colonialism). However, this began to change in the 1960s, when successive Commonwealth Immigrants Acts introduced immigration restrictions on a growing number of British subjects from outside the UK. Many Commonwealth citizens (including my maternal grandparents from Jamaica), were encouraged to come to Britain to fill jobs as bus drivers, nurses, midwives, ancillary workers, cleaners, cooks, and porters and other jobs available due to national labour shortages. Those who came were permitted to stay without time limit. When the Immigration Act 1971 came into force on 1 January 1973, the position of these Commonwealth citizens was preserved. Importantly, the Act preserved the right to come and go of those who had already arrived from their Commonwealth countries. The Immigration Act 1971 also recognised the right of their wives (not husbands) and children to join them. However, The Immigration Act 1988 changed that. Commonwealth citizens, like other people settled in the UK, would lose a right to remain indefinitely after two years absence.

The consequence of this action by the Home Office was that people from the Commonwealth, who had been encouraged to come to Britain to help the economy with a labour crisis, could not prove their citizenship. People who had left their communities, homes and families to come to Britain on the promise of a better life and to help rebuild the country, were deported and not permitted to come back. People were displaced from communities that were now home, lost their jobs, their homes, their right to access capital, mortgages, and loans, and became homeless. Racial disparities in housing have persisted for decades and are attributable in part to issues associated with migration and complex urban communities such as migrant networks and social capital, super-diversity, patterns of residence and transnationalism.

An impact of the immigration legislation is that two generations down from the Windrush scandal there are big differences in capital assets held across different racialised groups of people in UK society. Not only this, but the UK personal tax system provides tax benefits and tax penalties that also disproportionately impact on particular racialised groups. Byrne explains that the personal tax system in the UK is regressive on households: 'households are the significant economic unit for receipt of income and expenditure. It is inequality among households which matters, and the tax system is more or less flat across deciles of households, with the exception of the lowest decile, who pay the highest proportion of income as all tax of any decile.'[16] Between 2016–2019, over half of households from the Bangladeshi, Asian Other, Black and Other ethnic groups were in the two lowest income quintiles (after housing costs).[17]

This is a contemporary example of how societal context should not be separated from teachings of law and tax. This context is important in analysing computations of tax benefits from unearned income (e.g. property income) and personal tax computations in general, in understanding the nexus of law, tax and social context.

8.4 FURTHER CONTEXT TO CONSIDER WITHIN YOUR PRACTICE

Global reaching, socio-political, economic systems of colonialism and imperialism, continue to shape global law making and the context in which the law is applied. Colonialism typically involved the large-scale transfer of laws and legal institutions from one society to another, each of which had its own distinct sociocultural organisation and legal culture. The result was a dual legal

---

[16] David Byrne, 'Tax system does help cut inequality' (2019), available at @ theguardian .com/ money/ 2019/ may/ 29/ tax -system -doesnt -help -cut -inequality (accessed 3 October 2023).

[17] HMRC. Income distribution (2023), available at: ethnicity-facts-figures.service .gov.uk/work-pay-and-benefits/pay-and-income/income-distribution/latest (accessed 3 October 2023).

system: one for the colonised peoples and one for the colonisers. Dual legal systems were widespread in colonised parts of Africa, Asia, Latin America, and the Pacific. Postcolonial countries are now grappling with this legacy as they debate how to fashion a unified legal system out of this duality and how to resurrect and implement the remnants of indigenous, precolonial law.

For nearly 100 years, conventional comparative law scholars have classified a variety of broad transnational legal cultural characteristics into categories called families of law. Despite considerable disagreement about the theoretical bases and criteria for distinguishing such families, the concept has been and continues to be employed by many comparative scholars. Among the criteria utilised by families of law scholars during those eight decades were factors as diverse as ideology, legal technique, race, inherent attributes, historical antecedents, and legal style.[18]

As social awareness and attitudes towards race and the impact of racism have evolved in the UK, so too has legislation. The Race Relations Act 1965 was the first legislation in the UK to address racial discrimination. The Act outlawed discrimination on the 'grounds of colour, race, or ethnic or national origins' in public places in Great Britain. This ground-breaking anti-discrimination law was followed by the formation of the Race Relations Board in 1966. Evidence of racial discrimination in housing and employment continued after 1965 (as noted in the Windrush scandal referred to earlier in this chapter). The Race Relations Act 1976 finally extended the definition of discrimination to include indirect discrimination. Individuals who felt they had been discriminated against could take their complaints to the courts or industrial tribunals. The Act replaced the Race Relations Board with the Commission for Racial Equality, which was given greater powers of enquiry and enforcement.

Let's now move on from the societal context in which race discrimination legislation has evolved in the UK, to an exploration of the importance of integrating race as part of an anti-racist approach in law education.

8.5   ANTI-RACISM IN LAW EDUCATION

An anti-racist law education is one which is critical and inclusive. In practice, I suggest an anti-racist law education curriculum is one that:

- Acknowledges that peoples' ideologies and biases influence how they see the world.

---

[18] Konrad Zweigert and H. Hein Kötz, *An Introduction to Comparative Law* (tr Tony Weir, North-Holland Publ. Co., 1977) vol.1, pp. xvii, 385; vol. 2, pp. xvii, 379.

- Enables spaces of dialogue and enquiry to encourage students to see the world through the eyes of other people.
- Anchors the teaching of law in the social context in which it is formed or applied.
- Explores the history and patterns of power imbalances and discrimination within the law.
- Acknowledges the role that colonialism and imperialism have in the formation of structures e.g. families of law.
- Acknowledges that canons of law & epistemology of law is rooted in historical antecedents, of which ongoing systemic racism is an integral part.
- Acknowledges modern day systemic racism.

The next section of this chapter centres on practical activities you can focus on as part of an anti-racist, inclusive approach to law education.

8.6 CONVERSATIONS ABOUT RACE

Advance HE explain that an anti-racist curriculum recognises structural racism exists in our institutions and that power, privilege and elitism frame the curriculum through a White Eurocentric/Western perspective lens in our academic institutions.[19] A law curriculum that does not create spaces in which learners can reflect on their positionality in relation to what is centred as racially normative, that does not unveil the 'hidden curriculum' and associated problematic behaviours, that does not challenge, disrupt or make visible discrimination, is not an inclusive curriculum.

Students are not a homogeneous group. A huge challenge for educators is to provide a learning environment that meets the needs of all those in the learning environment. Tisdell (1995), argues inclusive learning environments should reflect the diversity of those present in the learning activity itself, in the curriculum and pedagogical style. When students do not see themselves in the content of the curriculum or its teaching, they experience a displacing dichotomy of hypervisibility and invisibility at the same time. This can be challenging for some students, as they struggle with the cognitive dissonance that may ensue. A response to this is code switching or muting of their opinion, perspectives, and voice. The mental gymnastics of being marginalised can be all consuming and exhausting. The importance of students having access to safe spaces to share their lived experience, to express their opinions, for dialogue and exchanging of ideas but also for contemplation, introspection and

---

[19] Advance HE, 'The anti-racist curriculum project' (2021), available at: advance-he.ac.uk/sites/default/files/2021-10/ARC%20Explained.pdf (accessed 3 October 2023).

reflection cannot be underestimated. Safety, and access to safe spaces to talk about race, is paramount.

You may feel you do not have the tools to talk about race or create the conditions of safety needed. Acknowledging this is a critical step. A starting point is to talk to colleagues who have expertise in providing psychological safe spaces e.g., health and well-being officers from professional services. This work also requires partnership approach with students themselves. Critical to conditions of safety is compassion and tolerance. Conversations about race can then take place within agreed boundaries that feel safe to those participating.

It is difficult work. The best work usually is. Each one of us working with students in education has a responsibility to do the work: it is a collective responsibility. As the educator, you will need to engage in an iterative process of introspection and reflection to better understand where you, the educator, are in your anti-racism journey. If you know you are not ready to enter into conversations about race or to bring a racialised lens into your teaching it is like any aspect of professional development needs: educate yourself, read, do some anti-racism training, ask others, attend webinars – but do the work.

Before an anti-racist pedagogical approach to law education is adopted, the spaces in which you interact with your students to talk about race should have an established level of psychological safety. Safety is temporal and different students will have differing levels of need, so regular check ins and modifications may be necessary. To create psychological safety in borderless spaces of engagement, takes intent, skill, compassion, time and scaffolding of boundaries. Creating conditions of psychological safety is part of the process of creating brave space.

Talking about race within the context of the curriculum and student experience can be transformative and contribute to the creation of inclusive culture. However, to talk about race effectively requires intentional, considered thought and action; compassion; and most of all that those engaging in conversations about race, feel safe. People need to enter into these conversations with compassion and care, particularly for those who are reliving trauma and lived experience during discussions about race but also for those who fear making mistakes. It is important you acknowledge that talking about race and racism may make people feel uncomfortable and may be triggering for some. This means it is not just safe spaces that are needed, it is actually brave space that needs to be created.

In brave spaces, there must be a shared understanding of intent; an openness and willingness to learn; to be compassionate and be accepting of mistakes; but also adopt a growth mindset to acknowledge and learn from those mistakes. There will undoubtedly be some level of disagreement and maybe even conflict which, as the educator in the space, you need to control. Controlled conflict is not a bad thing. As educators we need to frame conflict of opinion as a normal outcome of a diverse group. It is an important stage of developing critical thinking, and this will also be applicable to how the brave space may be curated by the educator and their students. Arao and Clemens suggest that it is important for participants in brave spaces to, 'own your intentions and your impact.'[20]

8.7 SOME PRACTICAL WAYS IN WHICH TO CREATE SAFE, BRAVE, ANTI-RACIST SPACE IN THE CLASSROOM

Developing anti-racist praxis and brave space can be very, very difficult. Learning spaces are transient and continuously evolve. I would suggest an incremental approach to the development of these spaces. There is no one size fits all approach. You may choose one thing initially to adopt e.g. when introducing a new piece of legislation into the programme, spending five minutes or so discussing the social context in which the legislation is situated. In another learning situation, you may choose to acknowledge and emphasise the impact of the legislation through a racialised lens. This progression from acknowledgement of race and racism through to discussion of its impact is not linear as it will work in some instances and not in others. The effectiveness of brave space is dependent on you the educator, but also on your students and their willingness to engage with their learning. All effective teaching requires creating conditions of trust, interest and enquiry; this is particularly true of anti-racist approaches to teaching and that's where I begin.

8.7.1 Provide Affective Environments of Enquiry and Interest

Get to know your students' names, their interests, their preferences, views, perspectives. This will happen through getting to know them. Provide open spaces for students to engage in dialogue or to experience solitude in their thinking. Spaces that may be timetabled, but undesignated, may also be important to allow planned unplanned discussions about race. These spaces can be used for confidence building and allow people into their space, for example by bringing in an aspect of conversation that was commented on by a student the previous week.

---

[20] Brian Arao and Kristie Clemens, *Confronting the paradox of safety in social justice education* (March 2006). Educational session presented at the annual meeting of ACPA College Student Educators International, Indianapolis, USA, available at: anselm.edu/sites/default/files/Documents/Center%20for%20Teaching%20Excellence/From%20Safe%20Spaces%20to%20Brave%20Spaces.pdf (accessed 3 October 2023).

Students will often gravitate towards people who are like them. This invariably means those students who are visually different will be marginalised. It is your responsibility as an educator to create an inclusive learning environment, where everyone is seen, acknowledged and feels included. You will need to use your expertise and lived experience as a former student to try and bring the community into the classroom.

Use learning spaces for peer led, group-based activities & discussion-based exchanges about views and critical thought, rather than to answer a question objectively. Perhaps discuss a discrimination case relating to graduate recruitment bias against a defendant with natural hair or discrimination case in relation to religion – discussions that students who are not usually seen in the curriculum feel empowered to comment on. Ideally, don't use this space to foster or reinforce hierarchies, just use it to bring in marginalised students if they choose to come into the space. Ask international students about the social context of their home country in relation to families of law being applied in the curriculum here. Allow for a diversity of voices in discussions.

A flipped learning approach is an excellent active learning approach that fosters an environment of enquiry and interest. A flipped learning approach is a pedagogical approach in which the conventional notion of classroom-based learning is inverted: students are introduced to the learning material before class with classroom time then being used to deepen understanding through discussion with peers and problem-solving activities facilitated by teachers.[21] Rather than adopting Socratic approaches to teaching e.g. didactic, 'chalk and talk' approaches to teaching, use the time you have with students in the classroom to encourage enquiry of thought, by applying and critiquing the principles of law and families of law. Encourage enquiry of thought by using case law to not only highlight principles of law, but to also support perspectives and views, or indeed to challenge expressed perspectives and views. Present a reasoned argument considering multiple perspectives and support these perspectives with research or evidence. It is important to acknowledge the validity of all expressed opinions as being held by those who offer them but use research or where appropriate learned/lived experience to support your assertions. After the class students can reflect upon the feedback they receive in class and use this to further their learning.

---

[21] National Teaching Fellow (2017), available at: advance-he.ac.uk/knowledge-hub/flipped-learning (accessed 3 October 2023).

8.7.2 Establish Safety Norms

Boundary setting should, wherever possible, be by consensus with your students. Use the lowest tolerance threshold of risk expressed by students as the boundary which everyone must adhere to. Boundaries may be values based, they may restrict sharing of personal information, they may provide physical boundaries to shared spaces: it is very much dependent on how students themselves will feel safe. A simple example of this is in group work. Some students, for example, are not happy to share personal contact details with other students. This should be established at the start of group work, by you as the educator, as a group norm. As the educator, you can normalise this by insisting that only official university contact details be shared amongst group members.

As the educator, you should ensure these boundaries of safety are constantly communicated and re-affirmed to all students, through module handbooks, on the virtual learning environment (VLE), messaging in lectures etc. In practice, this refers to the use of inclusive language; visual images used in different contexts (e.g., not re-affirming stereotyping of groups of students); positioning of narratives in discourse and chosen political figures or other individuals used to represent good/bad leaders in their practice; protagonists, oppressors, oppressed etc., associated with the programme. These actions will say much more to your students than your words or institutional strap lines about the parameters and conditions of safety to be experienced in your classroom.

The consequences of breaching the boundary norms should be established and agreed by everyone at the beginning of the course. As consensus within the group needs to be achieved, the framing of norms and their consequence will vary. It may be that you determine as a group there are no consequences, and everyone agrees to adhere to the norms in good faith. In other cases, for example, you may refer to existing student charters/disciplinary codes to frame the breach of boundary norms as misconduct. There may be some consequences deemed appropriate by you as the educator and your students that lie between these two actions e.g. penalties applied through peer scoring on a group assessment.

It is, however, very important not to conflate groupthink agreement with boundary norms. Setting norms is not about creating conditions that do not allow for difference of opinion, challenge or even conflict. It is just important that you create conditions in which all these things are controlled and understood by all.

Also, very importantly, students must be aware of health and well-being spaces they may wish to access during their learning. Discussing race can surface biases or trigger locked away experiences. The process can be a self-revelatory experience and it is critical that students know they have access to safe spaces to decompress, talk things through and deal with their emotions. Additionally, in setting boundaries and creating a safe environment in which to talk about race, all students must be made aware of the institutional race discrimination reporting policies and practices.

As is always the case, if students do not wish to engage in conversations about race, do not force them to. However, this should not prevent you as the educator, from adopting an anti-racist approach to your teaching and learning.

8.7.3 Show Vulnerability

Be open in sharing your anxieties in talking about race with your students. It is important to not put your emotional anxiety and the associated burden on your racially minoritised students. Be inclusive in these conversations, share your vulnerability and draw everyone in.[22] Use the space to encourage students to discuss the importance of tolerance when people get things wrong. Acknowledge people (including possibly yourself) will get things wrong. Everyone is on a journey when talking about race, and it is important people acknowledge mistakes will be made, this is an integral part of creating safe conditions. This is something that should be collectively acknowledged in creating and adopting brave space. Conditions in which it is safe to make mistakes, to agree to disagree on issues and to encourage tolerance and empathy is critical. In setting the conditions for controlled conflict, an important part of this is tolerance of learning by making mistakes. As the educator mediating this space, your role in doing this is vital. Everyone is an expert of their own experience. Those who have suffered racism, are the best placed to talk about racism, how it manifests in social structures and its impact. Of course, they should not carry the burden of educating the group, but their superior knowledge of this should be publicly acknowledged by the group.

There should, at the very least, be an agreement in setting the boundary norms to try not to invalidate the experiences of others. Where this happens, if it is pointed out by another student that they feel this has happened, your reaction should be compassion for all parties involved rather than anger. A mistake of this kind should be viewed as an opportunity for everyone to learn. Acknowledgement of the mistake, rather than a discussion of the impact of the mistake, may be what is agreed by you and the group in setting boundary norms, as the consequence. It may just be a statement of acknowledgment that 'your experience is not their experience, and we must respect that,' is said each time and it ends there.

Beyond acknowledgement of the mistake, it may well be that the norms relate to expectations around how people react to these issues and related

---

[22] See also Chapter 4.

mistakes (rather than a focus on prevention of these issues). You may have a collectively agreed broad principle, that where students seek to provide perspectives challenging historical truths presented to them in the context their learning e.g. the impact of the Immigration Act on the lived experience of migrants and access to housing, capital, wealth etc., they are encouraged to do so, but that no space is given for debate in the classroom. You may acknowledge the difference in opinion, reinforce the learning point (i.e. Immigration legislation has had a direct impact on access to wealth that has disproportionately impacted on some racially minoritised groups) together with the evidence being used in the teaching. It may then be that if you have allowed discussion and debate when setting the boundaries, that students are encouraged to offer evidence to support their perspectives. If no evidence is provided, a statement that 'your perspective on this matter is valid, but it is not supported with evidence' could be routinely given.

Finally, it is important to share any reservations you may have as an educator, whether it be as a white academic speaking about race, or as someone who does not have lived experience of these issues, with your students. The important thing for everyone is to acknowledge their position in relation to racism and agree whether acknowledgement of differences of opinion (notwithstanding those who experience racism being experts of their own experience) or whether the classroom is to be used as a safe, tolerant space of debate and learning (notwithstanding the fear, defensiveness. and vulnerability in doing so).

It may be that you stop at acknowledgment of racism rather than explore related issues because you do not have the tools to manage the brave space. Share this with the group, allow racially minoritised people to be acknowledged and seen, but keep them safe. Then do the learning to ensure that you can progress your anti-racist praxis.

8.7.4 Safety via Feedback

Re-affirm the importance of collective support and tolerance for all members of your learning community.[23] It is important to note these conditions of creating an anti-racist brave space are not one-off steps at the beginning of a module or unit, that then become self-perpetuating. Anti-racist approaches to teaching and learning requires continuous work. Feedback is essential to inform ongoing conversations and dialogue around the effectiveness and impact of the space. Informal feedback will probably be generated through interactions and discussions. However, perhaps consider having a few feedback points during

---

[23] See also Chapter 3.

the module/unit, that allow you to have a sense of how students feel about the anti-racist approach adopted.

Consider how to engage students in providing feedback. It may be that in setting boundary norms it was established that feedback about the use of an antiracist approach e.g. the use of case examples and discussion regarding racialisation of discrimination comes through a nominated individual(s), such as a class representative. Students may feel safer in providing feedback in other anonymous and/or informal ways e.g. Padlet or online quizzes/polls. Remember, students value the safety that anonymity can bring.

If students are identifiable in your feedback data, do not single them out in responding to feedback. It may be appropriate to speak to a student directly about their feedback, but do not expose them and their reflections publicly as this may make them feel unsafe. Of course, if a student vocalises their feedback in class, where appropriate it is good to respond directly. Safety of course, is paramount, so if responding to feedback requires time and space, communicate this to the student.

Do not feel you need to have the answers to everything, especially in the moment that feedback may be shared. Take time to be introspective and respond, rather than react.[24]

It is important to use dialogue to understand any issues and consider how the issues can be addressed. For example, students may acknowledge they like seeing themselves in the curriculum, but that they feel hyper-visible in lectures when asked to offer an opinion on an issue relating to race. Explore alternative approaches to waiting for responses from the class e.g. use an online, anonymous tool like Menitmeter to gather collective opinions on such a topic and then discuss them at a group, rather than individual, level.

You may consider a reverse mentoring approach as a structured way of getting feedback about your anti-racist approach. Adopting a reverse mentoring approach to getting feedback, breaks down power structures and is a signal to your students that you, as the educator, are in a position of learning. It can be empowering for the students who are engaged in the reverse mentoring relationship and offer another form of safety in the context of discussing issues associated with race.

8.8　YOU SEE ME, BUT DO YOU HEAR ME?

In creating safe, brave spaces, as part of an anti-racist approach to law education, it is imperative to note, different people experience safety in different

---

[24] See also Chapter 11.

ways. For some students, race is a fundamental part of who they are, for others not so.

'I don't see colour,' whilst perhaps well-meaning, is exclusionary. The blank canvas of colour-blindness ignores the gorgeous, rich tapestry of difference and diversity. Colour blindness strips racialised people (so called in this context, 'people of colour') of their presence in a racialised space. It is an active act of exclusion in which race is ironically ignored in the name of equality. We live in a racialised world. Race is socially constructed. The racialised category in which you are placed, based on skin colour (and other physical attributes), influences your positioning in the world by others e.g. framing you as 'disadvantaged' and consequently your lived experience and how you see the world.

I am a Black woman, and I will always be racialised as Black. However, my identity, who I am, my beliefs, my views, my perspectives, my societal role and positioning is developmental and transient. My identity is not fixed, but it is shaped and reinforced through education.

8.9 SUGGESTED ACTIONS

These proposed actions are for academic colleagues who are either relatively new to academia and/or at the start of their anti-racism learning.

1. **Engage in anti-racist learning** that meets your specific needs and circumstances to enable you to understand the different levels of racism (internalised, inter-personal, institutional, structural and systemic). Do not rely on racialised students or colleagues to educate you about racism. However, if they do, ensure that they are awarded recognition and credit for doing so.
2. **Racial literacy and articulating your social position using appropriate language** is important. Understanding and using the language of race is empowering and will provide you with more confidence to talk about race.
3. **Access support & shared learning** through internal/external networks of peers who focus on inclusive teaching praxis and engage in shared learning about the day-to-day realities of adopting inclusive/anti-racist praxis.
4. **Take ownership of your anti-racism learning** but do it with the understanding of the institutional context, culture, accepted norms, and tolerance thresholds for disruption, in which your developing anti-racist praxis is situated.
5. **Effectively protect yourself** through your support networks, mentors, allies, sponsors etc., from colleagues who seek to ensure you conform to existing 'colourblind' praxis to maintain that you do not disrupt the status quo.

6. **Set three simple realistic actions** you can carry out in an academic year to mitigate internalised and inter-personal racism e.g. use inclusive language in the classroom, co-create assessment with your students (including racially minoritised students), commit to learning and using all students' preferred names rather than imposing shortened, abbreviated or anglicised names.
7. **Share your intentions about your proposed actions with a trusted peer or someone in your network** and get feedback about the impact of these actions from someone trusted and appropriate e.g., racially minoritised peer. Accept it with humility and commit to making things better.
8. **Call out behaviour** that doesn't advance your commitment to tackle racism, and help individuals learn how to do better.
9. **Reflect on your actions**, the impact of these actions on you and others, and the feedback you have received.
10. **Be kind to yourself.** You alone cannot change systemic racism, but your actions can make a difference.

9. Wellbeing in the classroom

Georgina May Collins, Rita D'Alton-Harrison, David Yuratich

9.1 INTRODUCTION

For an academic who is engaged in teaching and who wants to build positive relationships with their students, it is important to consider how to promote student wellbeing. Our focus here is on how our teaching practices can be developed to promote student wellbeing in the classroom (including online and in-person teaching), and we do this by exploring three closely related themes:

1. How should you respond to confidential information about students relating to their sense of wellbeing?
2. How can you teach inclusively?
3. How can you respond to potential wellbeing issues as they arise within your classroom by 'noticing' potential problems and responding in an inclusive way?

We conceptualise wellbeing in two ways. In a broad sense, wellbeing in the classroom means tutors should promote the students' best interests through high quality teaching promoting other positive values, such as interactions with their peers and an enjoyable and supportive learning environment.[1] The classroom experience has the potential to shape how the student feels about themselves, their subject, the connections between their studies and their future career choices, and their sense of motivation.[2] In a narrower sense, promoting student wellbeing in the classroom means you should equip yourself with the tools and techniques needed to identify and respond to potential wellbeing issues as they arise, and to reduce the likelihood of them appearing

---

[1] Chi Baik, Wendy Larcome, and Abi Brooker, 'How universities can enhance student mental wellbeing: the student perspective' (2019) 38 Higher Education Research & Development 687, 683.

[2] Caroline Strevens and Clare Wilson, 'Law student wellbeing in the UK: a call for curriculum intervention' (2016) 11 JCLLE 44, 44–46.

later. As we now explain, a good way of doing is by looking at the classroom through the lenses of confidentiality, inclusivity, and noticing.

9.2 CONFIDENTIALITY AND STUDENT WELLBEING

It is likely one of the first times you will need to consider student wellbeing is when a student comes to you with information which they wish to remain confidential, or which you think should remain confidential (for ease, we will generally use 'confidential' to refer to all these situations). Confidential information will often raise a student wellbeing issue which can cross over into your in-class teaching practice. Think about this non-exhaustive list of student disclosures which we have encountered during our careers, each of which has an effect on student wellbeing potentially spilling over into the classroom:

- Being arrested.
- Being the victim of crime.
- Complaints about one of your colleagues.
- Concerns about their progress on a course.
- Family illness or bereavement.
- Financial difficulty.
- Mental and physical health problems.
- Neurodiversity.
- Specific learning difficulties ('SpLDs') such as dyslexia, dyspraxia, or ADHD.
- Substance abuse.

Sometimes confidential information will not require you to do much (or anything) to adapt your classroom practice. Say a bereavement has caused the student to fall behind, or they face financial hardship. These two conversations may be emotive, but they do not necessarily flow into the classroom. You can probably help the student catch up and should be able to find out about any financial support offered by your institution. Often, though, it may be less clear how to respond. Our focus is going to be on how confidential information affects your practice in the classroom, but it is also important to bear in mind when you need to escalate such information because it has deeper student wellbeing implications.

9.3 ESCALATING CONFIDENTIAL INFORMATION

Not all confidential information truly is confidential, in that it genuinely cannot, or need not, be shared. Sometimes a student, if asked, may be happy for you to share the information with a small group (such as other lecturers in that year, or careers/placement providers). At other times you may want to keep a student's confidence, but that must be balanced against what is best for the student and whether it is appropriate or necessary to seek further support by involving institutional welfare processes. For example, if a student is upset by changes in their personal life, that information might not need to be shared within the wider university; but if a student has expressed suicidal ideation, that information must be escalated as soon as possible.

Universities do not owe a general duty of confidentiality to students, but they do owe them a duty of care in certain situations and have obligations arising under the student contract.[3] Data protection law allows information about student health (or other confidential information) to be shared in certain circumstances, particularly if it is an urgent situation, and other laws may also require certain matters to be shared with third parties.[4] The law is complex and institutional procedures vary. It is essential you familiarise yourself with your institution's policies, including what sort of information can and should be escalated and how you should document your interactions with students. If in doubt, ask more experienced colleagues for advice without identifying the student.

Receiving confidential information can come as a shock and may be upsetting or even traumatising. Remember, wellbeing cuts both ways: when we think about wellbeing in a law school, we are not only talking about student wellbeing, and you should seek out support if you need it.[5]

All that said, our focus is narrow: it is the effect that the receipt of confidential information has for the protection of student wellbeing within the classroom. Our attention now shifts to how your knowledge of confidential information affects your classroom practice.

---

[3] Jim Dickinson, 'What does duty of care mean when it comes to universities and students?' (*WonkHE*, 22 May 2023), available at: wonkhe.com/blogs/what-does-duty-of-care-mean-when-it-comes-to-universities-and-students/ (accessed 3 October 2023). As this book was going to press, the High Court was due to hear Bristol University v Abrahart, which may determine the scope of a university's duty of care to its students. Readers should refer to the judgment for guidance on duties of care towards students.

[4] Viv Adams, 'Sharing personal data in an emergency – a guide for universities and colleges' (*ICO.org,* 14 September 2021), available at: ico.org.uk/about-the-ico/media-centre/blog-sharing-personal-data-in-an-emergency-a-guide-for-universities-and-colleges (accessed 3 October 2023).

[5] See Chapter 2.

9.4 CONFIDENTIAL INFORMATION AND CLASSROOM TEACHING

Some disclosures will not require specific actions within the classroom, beyond being generally sympathetic to the student's contributions, particularly if you know their preparation has been affected by an ongoing problem. As we explain later, being empathetic and understanding of students is in general an important factor in promoting student wellbeing.[6] In fact, most of what we will discuss can be applied to non-confidential student disclosures. There is no reason why confidential information is inherently more problematic or serious than non-confidential information; many students will be vocal about the challenges they are facing. Perhaps the key difference is that when you have received confidential information there is sometimes greater emphasis on acting with discretion and empathy.

As noted above, if the problem seems to be particularly serious, it should be escalated in accordance with your institution's policies. Nonetheless, escalation by itself is not the same thing as adapting your classroom practices in a way that helps to mitigate the student wellbeing issues which are linked to the confidential disclosure. It can be helpful to think through these inter-related factors when considering whether to change your approach to teaching in light of the disclosure:

9.4.1 Impact on Student Participation

Does the disclosure reveal something which could impact the student's ability (or their classmates' ability) to prepare for or participate in class? If so, what is that impact and how might it (reasonably) be mitigated? It might be appropriate to discuss this with the affected students, so long as you do not think doing so will harm their wellbeing; seek further advice if necessary. Some examples are:

- If a student has not been able to prepare effectively or is not in a position to contribute, do not call on them to speak during class. This does not mean the student will not participate; students with anxiety, for example, may prefer to contribute on their own terms, and a student who has not done the reading may be able to provide insightful comments during the class.
- Giving a content/trigger warning. For example, if a student has recently terminated a pregnancy and an upcoming class will discuss abortion, that

---

[6] Baik, Larcome, and Brooker (n 1) 680. For discussion of student wellbeing support see Chapter 3 and Chapter 4.

student may appreciate knowing this in advance, particularly if the discussion is not predictable. The warning could be a private one aimed at an individual student, or you might consider issuing a class-wide statement. The purpose of the warning is to ensure students have the information needed to mentally prepare themselves for class and to retain a sense of agency over how they engage with their education.[7] If the class is particularly important – e.g. if it is linked to assessment – this should be clearly explained.

- If the information signposts a long-term absence or lack of participation from the student, then direct them to sources of academic support such as your office hours. This is in addition to any escalation to pastoral support services and potentially periodically checking in with the student.

9.4.2 Impact on Your Lesson Plan(s) and Module Aims

Do the identified mitigations require you to change how you plan to run a session? For example:

- If a student has been diagnosed with an SpLD or is neurodivergent, and you had planned in an upcoming class for that student to give a non-assessed presentation or to read materials aloud, it may be appropriate to change your plans.
- If you had planned group work, and the student has disclosed they have recently ended a relationship with a student in the same class, you may need to ensure the students are not placed in the same group.
- If you are keen for all students to participate, but you know one or more students cannot, are there other ways you could include them? You could offer to discuss the materials in office hours or consider using an online engagement tool which allows students to respond to questions or tasks in advance, although care should be taken with online tools because they can cause accessibility issues. Inclusive teaching, as we discuss later, is good teaching.[8]

That said, it may be best to discuss your plans and the student's individual access needs with the student (and you should always speak to the EDI

---

[7] Kim D. Chanbonpin, 'Crisis and Trigger Warnings: Reflections on Legal Education and the Social Value of the Law' (2015) 90 Chi-Kent L Rev 615, 631–33; Michelle Bentley, 'Trigger Warnings and the Student Experience' (2017) 37 Politics 470, 470. See also Chapter 6.

[8] Cf. Samantha Ahern, 'Compassionate Pedagogy in Practice' (*UCL Digital Education Blog*, 3 July 2019).

or disability lead, or equivalent, in your department), because even the most well-intended intervention may leave the student feeling patronised or singled-out. They may not want or need anything to change, or you may have misunderstood the appropriate reasonable accommodations. You must also recognise that sometimes change is not appropriate or possible, and if so, should explain this to the student. An obvious area here is assessment, which is usually not something that can change at short notice, although do make sure you consult with colleagues who have responsibility for assessments before making any definitive statements about assessment adjustments.

9.4.3 Can You Make Long-term Changes?

Our discussion so far reflects that, in general, you will receive and need to act on confidential information from students in a reactive way. However, this fire-fighting approach is not the only way to adapt your classroom practice to promotes student wellbeing. Take time to reflect on how you have responded to confidential information. Reflective practice is important; a good teacher is a self-critical and reflective one who will actively learn lessons from what has or has not gone well.[9] If you are leading a module, or have a voice within a module leadership team, it is wise to consider how its curriculum can support wellbeing more broadly. For example:

- Is your course and assessment design sufficiently flexible that it can adapt, if needed, to any unexpected challenges or student needs?
- Is it appropriate to insert specific activities or resources into the course or programme which are designed to promote student wellbeing, such as those designed to help students deal with stress, improve their motivation, or promote a sense of community?[10]
- Could the volume of work on your course undermine student wellbeing? As Bleasdale and Humphreys put it: 'what needs to be difficult and why?'[11]

---

[9] Rachel Spencer, '"Hell is Other People": Rethinking the Socratic Method for Quiet Law Students' (2022) 56 Law Teacher 90.
[10] Stella Coyle and Hannah Gibbons-Jones, '"Make glorious mistakes!" Fostering growth and wellbeing in HE transition' (2022) 56 Law Teacher 37; Strevens and Wilson (n 2). See also Chapter 9.
[11] Lydia Bleasdale and Sarah Humphreys, 'Undergraduate Resilience Research Project: Executive Summary' (Leeds Institute for Teaching Excellence, 2018), available at: teachingexcellence .leeds .ac .uk/ wp -content/ uploads/ sites/ 89/ 2017/ 11/ LF _reportexec_sumbleasdale-humphreys.pdf (accessed 3 October 2023).

9.5 INCLUSIVITY AND STUDENT WELLBEING

Inclusivity can build trust, reduce uncertainty, and create a sense of belonging.[12] It is a recognition and celebration of student diversity that should influence teaching. It has the potential to transform the classroom environment into one which promotes positive student wellbeing. Inclusivity in the teaching and learning context seeks to create an environment in which all students are able to learn and in which their experience and diversity has value.[13]

Most institutions have processes/policies in place which attempt to ensure inclusivity. However, there are numerous elements of inclusive practice that remain unwritten. These processes often require students to inform us of their circumstances, or to actively reach out for assistance, recognising they need this help before they reach crisis point or disengage from their studies. There are those whose wellbeing concerns may not have triggered, or be appropriately captured by, university adjustment policies. To assist these students, we must adopt an inclusive approach.

Ensuring students feel valued and included, and community building, avoids the 'social pain' that can arise when students feel devalued, or experience feelings of exclusion and rejection.[14] This in turn enables them to engage more easily with the learning environment. One theme running throughout this section is the negative impact uncertainty can have on student wellbeing, and how adopting an inclusive approach assists in alleviating, and at times accepting, this uncertainty.

Adopting methods that work well for you and your students will take time. This is part of the reflective practice that should underpin inclusive practice, ensuring 'pedagogy, curricula and assessment are designed to engage students in learning that is meaningful, relevant, and accessible to all.'[15]

---

[12] See also Chapter 4.

[13] Ivan Figueroa, 'The Value of Connectedness in Inclusive Teaching' in Thomas Cornell (ed), *Inclusive Teaching: Presence in the Classroom: New Directions for Teaching and Learning, Number 140* (John Wiley & Sons, 2014) 46. See also Chapter 8.

[14] Zhansheng Chen and Kipling D. Williams, 'Social Pain is Easily Relived and Prelived, but Physical Pain is Not' in Geoff MacDonald and Laurie Jensen-Campbell (eds), *Social Pain: Neuropsychological and health implications of loss and exclusion* (American Psychological Association, 2011) 163. Cf. Jan McArthur, 'Assessment for Social Justice: The Role of Assessment in Achieving Social Justice' (2016) 41(7) Assessment & Evaluation in Higher Education 967–81 and Jan McArthur, *Assessment for Social Justice* (Bloomsbury, 2018).

[15] Christine Hockings, *Inclusive learning and teaching in higher education: A synthesis of research* (Higher Education Academy, 2010) 1.

9.6 INCLUSIVE DESIGN AND DELIVERY

Inclusive curriculum design and delivery requires us to build student support into the course. In the first instance we should ensure reasonable adjustments have been made, and materials are accessible. However, there are a number of other elements that go beyond this baseline. The first is bringing together academic and pastoral support. As Meyers states, 'students care if we care about them.'[16] Signpost student support in your handbook and make repeated references to this throughout the year, particularly during stressful times (e.g. assessment periods). This positions pastoral support and positive student wellbeing as a valuable element of the academic subject you are delivering and reinforces that you are a 'caring teacher.' Emphasise that their wellbeing takes priority and encourage them to reach out for support when needed. This builds a positive staff-student relationship; you're an 'approachable academic' who they feel comfortable asking for support.

In considering how we deliver (and design) our courses we must acknowledge 'the terror that uncertainty creates in students.'[17] Of course a degree of uncertainty is expected, and learning how to deal with uncertainty is a key skill. Uncertainty may arise in relation to knowledge: 'I don't know the *right* answer', and often more importantly 'everyone else does'. Or it may instead be about process: 'I don't know what I'm supposed to do', 'how do I do *all* this reading?' In either case those uncertainties negatively impact student wellbeing.[18] Informing students how the course will run, what seminars are for and how we conduct them, and what our expectations are can be reassuring.[19]

We should emphasise it's ok not to 'have the right answer', indeed often there isn't one! Embracing this uncertainty and encouraging students to challenge the material can not only help students become more critical thinkers, but can also be an excellent way of considering whether our curriculum is diverse. Whose texts do we recommend, and do we offer critiques from a variety of

---

[16] Steven Meyers, 'Do your students care whether you care about them?' (2009) 57(4) College Teaching 205, 206. See also Chapter 4.

[17] Fiona Donson and Catherine O'Sullivan, 'Building Block or Stumbling Block? Teaching Actus Reus and Mens Rea in Criminal Law' in Kris Gledhill and Ben Livings, *The Teaching of Criminal Law: The Pedagogical Imperatives* (Routledge, 2016) 7.

[18] On uncertainty and the impact it can have on student mental health, see Gareth Hughes et al, *Education for Mental Health Enhancing Student Mental Health through Curriculum and Pedagogy* (Advance HE, 8 February 2022), available at: advance-he.ac.uk/teaching-and-learning/curricula-development/education-mental-health-toolkit (accessed 3 October 2023).

[19] See Gareth Hughes, *Be Well, Learn Well: Improve your wellbeing and academic performance* (Macmillan, 2020) and Paul Penn, *The Psychology of Effective Studying: How to succeed in your Degree* (Routledge, 2019).

perspectives? Engaging in decolonisation work and embracing criticality in the classroom plays a central role in creating an inclusive learning environment. We can introduce students to critical views, and invite them to challenge them based on their experiences and perspectives. From there we might recommend reading building on this, and use this to inform future recommended texts, contributing to curriculum diversification. In continuing to diversify and decolonise the curriculum we can also 'co-produce knowledge' with our students drawing on their diverse experiences.[20] This creates a classroom community in which students feel a sense of belonging, where they are able to challenge and dismantle dominant 'knowledge.'[21] The choices we make in the classroom, including what perspectives we give value to in our courses, 'convey messages and values which may reach well beyond those of the particular learning tasks which give a lesson its formal focus.'[22]

Often, as academics, we seem as though we know everything. We're confident learners and teachers, and we have all the answers. Of course, for most of us that's not entirely true. Where we openly admit the challenges we faced as a learner, students see us as human. We can not only demonstrate empathy, but we can also show students how we went from a place of confusion or uncertainty to being confident enough to teach them how to do that too. If for example, there is a particular concept that took you time to understand, explain how you broke it down, show them your process. Did you use diagrams, or rely on particular resources? Share these with your students and take them on that same journey with you. When doing so, be honest about why you're adopting that approach – because you understand how some of them will feel because you felt that way too, perhaps not even that long ago! For students, seeing academics that are 'like them' is invaluable. However, what is equally important is discovering that academics are like them, that they understand and empathise with them.

Where we are very clear about the purpose of seminars not being to answer 'why of course it's X' but rather to consider how we got to X, questioning or critiquing X, or whether it's X at all, this enhances students' critical thinking and their engagement with the teaching and learning process, and makes them

---

[20] Ahmed Raza Memon and Suhraiya Jivraj, 'Trust, courage and silence: carving out decolonial spaces in higher education through student–staff partnerships' (2020) 54(4) The Law Teacher 475, 481. See also Chapter 9.

[21] Cf. Jason Arday, Dina Zoe Belluigi and Dave Thomas, 'Attempting to break the chain: reimaging inclusive pedagogy and decolonising the curriculum within the academy' (2021) 53(3) Race, Equality and Social Mobility in Education 298–313.

[22] Robin Alexander, 'Border crossings: towards a comparative pedagogy' (2001) 37(4) Comparative Education 507, 515. See also Chapter 8.

confident learners who understand what is expected of them, who accept and perhaps even enjoy uncertainty.

9.7 THE APPROACHABLE ACADEMIC

A welcoming learning environment and positive student-tutor relationship are essential features of the inclusive classroom and play a significant part in positive student wellbeing.[23] They have the ability to improve academic engagement and attainment. They can also help to ease the aforementioned uncertainty that can make students reluctant to engage. But how do we create these relationships?

When we arrive in the classroom it's important we start by prioritising the class environment before diving into the substantive content. It's useful to start with introductions, encouraging students to engage with their peers inside and outside the classroom. Establishing this sense of community assists in creating a sense of belonging and makes students more invested in the group learning experience.[24] Providing an overview of classroom expectations or seminar etiquette allows us to ease students' uncertainties. Inform them this is a space where they can and should ask questions, where they're not expected to know the 'right' answer, where their opinions and perspectives are of value, and that you are here to support them.[25]

There are numerous ways we can signal our approachability, and that helps students feel welcome and able to engage in the teaching and learning process.[26] This includes: the use of humour, giving students the opportunity to discuss their opinions and perspectives, and providing positive and constructive feedback. Learning and using students' names is a powerful tool rather than a simple courtesy. It creates a sense of belonging and shows we care about them not only as students but also as people: it's key to relationship building.[27] Non-verbal actions play a huge role in cultivating a welcoming learning environment and relationship building: these include eye contact, smiling and

---

[23] Cf. Karen Seary and Julie Willans, 'Pastoral Care and the Caring Teacher – Value Adding to Enabling Education' (2020) 11(1) Student Success 12–21.

[24] Michael Fay and Yvonne Skipper, '"I was able to ask for help when I became stressed rather than sitting alone and struggling": psychology and law students' views of the impact of identity and community on mental wellbeing' (2022) 56(1) The Law Teacher 20–36.

[25] See also Chapter 8.

[26] See also Chapter 6.

[27] See e.g., the 'Say My Name' Project, available at: warwick.ac.uk/services/dean-of-students-office/community-values-education/saymyname/ (accessed 3 October 2023).

nodding, and breaking up the session by moving around and interacting with individual students or small groups.

In creating meaningful relationships with students, we 'can begin to address the lack of belongingness experienced and heightened anxiety' experienced by many.[28] The uncertainty underpinning this has strong links with the 'fear of "failing"', and concerns raised by students in relation to contributing to seminars. Uncertainty in the degree experience is expected. Normalising this uncertainty, because we as learners felt the same, might assist in creating an environment where students feel comfortable contributing and thinking creatively. This can be as simple as being open about our own experiences, or we might actively encourage students to 'make glorious mistakes' whilst 'smuggling' wellbeing messages into the teaching environment.[29] This 'smuggling' might include asking students how they are, or checking whether students are quiet because the content is difficult or because it's 9am on a Monday! This works well alongside more overt messaging such as signposting sources of support.

It's important we are not only approachable in theory but accessible in practice. Of course, we must be mindful of boundaries, workload etc. As such, in emphasising the importance of responsiveness and availability we are not suggesting that academics should be *constantly* available. Instead, what is important is that students know how to contact us, and when they can expect a response. We should be clear about the role of office hours, let students know if you're happy for them to drop in, again helping to alleviate the uncertainty surrounding and university 'norms'.

9.8 THE ROLE OF ASSESSMENT AND FEEDBACK

Linked to inclusive design is the significant impact both assessment and feedback can have on student wellbeing. In addition to ensuring the assessment is inclusive,[30] and reinforcing the importance of seeking academic and pastoral support, there are further considerations that might be made. Although it's

---

[28] Natalie Skead and Shane Rogers, 'Stress, Anxiety and Depression in Law Students: How Student Behaviours Affect Student Wellbeing' (2014) 40(2) Monash University Law Review 564, 586.

[29] Coyle and Gibbons-Jones (n 10) 37, 48.

[30] Emma Allen, 'Not a Moot Point! Mooting as an Authentic Assessment Practice in Law?' (2021) 13 The Journal of Academic Development and Education 50–53. On assessment and wellbeing see: Wendy Larcombe et al, 'Does an Improved Experience of Law School Protect Students against Depression, Anxiety and Stress: An Empirical Study of Wellbeing and the Law School Experience of LLB and JD Students' (2013) 35 Sydney L. Rev. 407.

important we provide support and information around assessment periods, this is something we should also integrate into the course as a whole, and we should tell students this is what we have done. The classroom should be a space where we talk openly about the purpose of the assessment, our expectations, and what support is available. We should tell our students the seminars have prepared them for their assessment(s), so they can approach these with confidence. We should be clear feedback is an ongoing process, the conversations we have in the classroom are just as important 'formal' feedback.

Providing students with formative assessments helps them prepare for summative assessments, can alleviate feelings of uncertainty and build students' confidence.[31] There are of course often constraints on how much we can do in relation to assessment. However, there are still ways of providing formative 'assessment' and building feedback into the course to support students' learning and wellbeing.[32] For example, if seminars match the assessment and students receive an opportunity to test their knowledge and skills in every session – tell them. Knowing they have done this task before, and have received positive and constructive feedback, is hugely worthwhile. Further, you can consider how seminars can be more explicitly tailored to assessment. For example, could one seminar involve students looking at past papers and then receiving feedback from staff and their peers? Techniques like these allow us to provide students with the support and feedback they need whilst recognising the pressures on our time.

In the midst of marking it can be easy to slip into assumptions about a lack of effort, preparation, or even ability. However, prepare feedback with care. We need to remember what we have seen (and built) in the classroom and drop those assumptions. Instead, we should use feedback as another opportunity to signpost support. If several students have fallen into the same 'trap' we ought to consider whether our expectations were explicit. *How* did this issue arise

---

[31] Cf. Jacqueline Leighton and María Clara Bustos Gómez, 'A pedagogical alliance for trust, wellbeing and the identification of errors for learning and formative assessment' (2018) 38(3) Educational Psychology 381–406; Ann-Marie Houghton and Jill Anderson, *Embedding Mental Wellbeing in the Curriculum: Maximising Success in Higher Education* (HEA, 2017) 23, available at: advance-he.ac.uk/knowledge-hub/embedding-mental-wellbeing-curriculum-maximising-success-higher-education (available 3 October 2023).

[32] See the discussion of constructive alignment in: John Biggs and Catherine Tang, *Teaching for Quality Learning at University: What the Student Does* (4th edn, Open University Press, 2011). On assessment and feedback, see David Carless and David Boud, 'The development of student feedback literacy: enabling uptake of feedback' (2018) 43(8) Assessment & Evaluation in Higher Education 1315–25, and Naomi Winstone and David Carless, *Designing Effective Feedback Processes in Higher Education: A Learning-Focused Approach* (Taylor & Francis, 2019).

and is there something that can be done to prevent it in the future? It is an opportunity for us to reflect as much as it is for our students.

Where, as 'approachable academics', we have consistently adopted a caring approach and constructed a supportive narrative, students are more receptive of, and able to engage with, feedback.[33] Feedback works both ways. Ensuring students know we are open to ongoing feedback, that we are happy to adjust or explain our approach, is of huge value in the context of relationship building. What students say when thinking about assessment also provides us with an opportunity for reflection. For example, if a student asks: 'what happens if I fail the assignment/module/course?' of course this can be an opportunity to explain the relevant processes and such. However, more importantly consider *why* they're asking that question, why do they not feel confident in their abilities: is it the academic content or is something more going on? What support do they need? We should use this feedback, our observations, and our experiences to further enhance our teaching practice, ensure inclusivity, and in turn promote positive student wellbeing.

9.9 NOTICING

Arguably one of the most important aspects of classroom teaching is observation but what is key to promoting student wellbeing and inclusivity is what we notice from observations of both the student and classroom environment. Mason[34] defines 'noticing' as the act of focusing a tutor's attention in order to raise awareness. Mason argues that whilst we can learn from experience, we cannot experience without noticing.[35] Noticing allows us to appreciate what we know or don't know, or what we need to experience and respond to. Noticing is therefore the important bridge to reflecting on our teaching practices and can also be an important mechanism for identifying student wellbeing issues.

9.9.1 Noticing Classroom Interaction

In order to ensure important things do not go unnoticed we also need to understand how to recognise clues. In a classroom setting there can be many clues arising in a single teaching session that impact on wellbeing. Let's consider

---

[33] See e.g., Naomi Winstone et al, 'Supporting learners; agentic engagement with feedback: A systematic review and taxonomy of recipience processes' (2016) 52(1) Educational Psychologist 1–21.

[34] John Mason, *Researching Your Own Practice: The Discipline of Noticing* (Routledge, 2002) 7.

[35] Ibid, 30.

the following as an example – the advice applies equally to online/virtual classroom as well as in-person traditional classroom settings:

9.9.1.1 Fictional scenario

The tutor is taking a group of first year undergraduate students for their first seminar. The tutor arrives to find ten students all seated at tables but sitting apart from each other. The tutor introduces themselves. The tutor then starts addressing the seminar topic. During the session a further four students arrive five minutes late. The tutor continues speaking and asks for the answer to one of the seminar questions, but nobody responds. The tutor changes direction and asks individual questions to individual students. Some students are able to answer but one student (student A) is unable to answer and looks at the floor. Student A is wearing several layers although there is a heatwave. Another student (student B) is scrolling on her phone. All other students have laptops. Halfway during the session student C leaves the classroom and returns five minutes later, apologising for leaving. The tutor turns their back to the class to write on the board and continues talking with their back to the students (or camera off) for five minutes. When the tutor turns around, they find that student D is looking out the window and the tutor suspects they have not been engaged for the entire five minutes, although they had previously been participating in the session. The tutor then asks students to engage in a group exercise and selects student E to write a summary of the discussion on the board/virtual whiteboard. Student E refuses, saying they have terrible handwriting.

The above scenario highlights a number of important issues related to how students are experiencing the session intellectually, and highlights possible student wellbeing issues. Consider what the tutor should have been able to notice and what may be less obvious but nonetheless still holds some clues about the need for enquiry.

One of the early 'noticing clues' in the above scenario is the lack of student interaction and engagement. This is not unusual given that this is their first seminar, and they will be unfamiliar with the classroom, the tutor and their classmates. This becomes an important clue for a tutor even before they have entered the classroom. Whether an online or in-person session, the tutor could have designed some 'ice-breaker' activities to introduce an informal and friendly environment. Examples might involve asking the students to introduce themselves by saying a few words about themselves or their decision to come to university. Ideally a tutor should aim to become acquainted with the names of all students in their class together with any recorded declared disabilities. This can be achieved with the assistance of photographs and information from a central student dashboard. However, sometimes disabilities may be undeclared or unseen. A tutor should therefore never assume they are dealing with a homogeneous group simply labelled 'students.' Each student is an individual with individual needs and may have a history that will not always be known to the tutor. Yet a tutor needs to be able to respond to any perceived needs even when these are not voiced.

Alternatively, the tutor could have prepared some simple interactive welcoming activities for the students before launching into the teaching session. Examples include asking students to identify their role models with reasons why (in the case of a virtual classroom students might use photos, emojis or avatars for visual representations of role models), playing a simple game of 'meet and greet' by alternating chairs, or in the case of online activities using breakout rooms to alternate students into spaces to introduce themselves to each other and so on. However, tutors should be mindful of any accessibility or learning needs of students in the room when devising these activities.

Once in the classroom the tutor should have noticed the lack of familiarity by observing the students had chosen to sit at separate tables. In an online session this lack of familiarity or engagement might be signalled by the fact that students have their cameras turned off. One area where a tutor is in control is in relation to their teaching style and methods, so a tutor should notice when certain methods are not working and be prepared to adapt. This may involve trying different techniques for different cohorts. In a virtual classroom (where technology and bandwidth permit) a tutor should ideally keep their own camera on, as facial expressions and body language also serve to underline and reinforce messages and support the delivery of teaching. A tutor should be mindful there may be students relying on lipreading and so turning their back to the classroom or turning off cameras is not an inclusive way to teach. Whilst the virtual classroom will often have 'word capture' that allows speech to be translated into text, not all words are captured correctly.

Teaching sessions should create a learning environment that allows for flexibility, the integration of different resources and broad range of activities.[36] The layout of the classroom could have been adjusted: For example, the tutor could ask students to come together on a single large table, perhaps with the tutor at the head of the table. Even where circumstances prevent close contact, bringing students together socially (if not physically) would immediately have lifted the mood in the classroom. In the case of a virtual classroom this could be achieved through the use of so-called 'breakout rooms' that enable small groups of students to be separated together in one virtual space to hold a discussion.

---

[36] See e.g., Noel M. Meyers and Duncan D. Nulty, 'How to use (five) curriculum design principles to align authentic learning environments, assessment, students' approaches to thinking and learning outcomes' (2009) 34(5) Assessment and Evaluation in Higher Education; John B. Biggs, *Teaching for Quality at University* (2nd edn, Open University, 2003).

The session is then interrupted by the lateness of five students. Whilst a tutor could demand an immediate explanation and apology from these students, a public confrontation often serves to alienate the students or temporarily damage the tutor-student relationship. This does not mean the lateness should go unnoticed or unchallenged. The students should initially be asked to settle themselves quickly and participate in the session. However, after the session the tutor should ask the students to stay behind to establish the reason for their lateness. It may be these students were released from a previous session late, or that they were initially unable to find the classroom, or that they were confused about their timetable. There may be other reasons such as the fact the students are commuting to the institution from their family home rather than being in student accommodation. This offers an opportunity for the tutor to give students guidance and support rather than a reprimand.

The next issue the tutor could have addressed was question handling. Whilst all students are expected to participate during a session, students can often feel uncomfortable testing their knowledge and understanding for the first time amongst strangers. Providing general encouragement before posing questions could have put students at ease. For example, publicly recognising the seminar group is a support group where individuals will learn from each other and that whilst all students will invariably get things wrong in their answers, the seminars are a safe space to make mistakes. Students need to be given the message they should come prepared and ready to participate, not that they must always answer each question correctly. After all, if they were able to do that, they would not require the services of their tutor.

The tutor in our scenario asked students to volunteer to provide an answer to the first seminar question. This is likely to attract responses from confident students, but not the less confident ones. Instead, if the question was a complex one, the tutor could have broken it into segments and asked students to volunteer to start a group discussion that would help the group to build an answer, rather than one student tackling the whole answer by themselves. This would ease students into the discussion, rather than making them feel the spotlight is solely upon them. This is not to say students should never be asked to tackle a full answer on their own. The expectation is students will become proficient in speaking in front of an audience and justifying their responses and interpretations of the question. However, to build trust and confidence a tutor may need to approach this ultimate goal in stages.

Asking questions to individual students as a way to establish which students have understood and which students are still struggling with concepts is acceptable. However, as seen in the case of student A, this may not always be appropriate. Rather than moving on to the next student the tutor could have tried ways to simplify the question or ask the student to answer from a 'world view' or personal opinion perspective to generate some thought or debate that does not rely on the student having done their pre-reading. This ensures the student is not unintentionally named and shamed due to their failure to answer, and that they feel included in the discussions around the topic. Hopefully this sustains their interest and engagement for the remainder of the session.

Where a student is unable to answer, as was the case with student A, this may signal they are unprepared, which in turn may hold clues to possible student wellbeing issues. Another clue is the fact the student is wearing several layers during a heatwave. There could be an undisclosed trauma affecting this student and body language such as avoiding eye contact, sitting alone, being overly nervous or aggressive could be confirmatory of this. Students who are self-harming will hide these signs by using additional clothing to conceal this physical trauma. If the tutor is not the student's personal tutor, they should mention any concerns they have to the student's personal tutor and ask them to speak with the student to check on their wellbeing. However, as a classroom tutor then action can be taken by noting the student was unprepared and checking in the next seminar whether this has changed. If it remains an issue, the tutor should consider a private discussion with the student. Unprepared students may turn into absent students if they fear being asked to participate in sessions. If a student has ongoing personal or health problems impacting on their time, engagement or participation, a referral should be made to the appropriate institutional wellbeing services and a discussion about interrupting their studies may be warranted if it becomes a continuing issue.

The tutor notices student C is scrolling on their phone but does not know why. It would be easy to assume the student is distracted, perhaps searching on the internet or using social media. It would be a normal impulse and perhaps logical to ask the student to put their phone away. However, there may be another explanation: the phone may be a cheaper replacement for a laptop. The student may in fact be engaged in the lesson and be scrolling to find the seminar questions or their pre-prepared answer. The tutor could test whether the phone is a legitimate educational aid by wandering around the classroom as they speak, glancing at each student's notes including student C. If student C responds by putting their phone away, this might indeed suggest they are involved in activities they do not want the tutor to see. However, if the phone is left visible this may suggest it is being used as a technological aid to learning. In the case of a virtual classroom environment the tutor could simply send a private message to the student through the relevant online teaching platform to check they need to use the phone or simply say to all students that there is no need to use any additional technology for the moment as all materials or information will be posted on the teaching platform.

A tutor needs to be careful about how they address this issue. If they choose to do so at the end of the session, then seeking a simple clarification that the mobile phone is being used for learning purposes during the sessions may be sufficient. The use of a mobile phone may be an individual choice or there may be an issue around access to technology due to financial constraints. A student is unlikely to be able to write a full essay with any required referencing styles on a mobile phone. The tutor should use the opportunity to remind the student of the location of computer suites if needed as well as any student financial assistance packages. The right study space and access to technical support were the two biggest deficiencies identified by the Barber Report[37] that looked at the shift from traditional teaching methods towards digital teaching and learning.

Student D disengages at the point the tutor begins to write on the board. Whilst a tutor should be aware of all students with declared disabilities in their classroom, not all institutions share disability and dyslexic information widely and not all students declare (or are aware of) their unseen disabilities. As such a tutor should proceed on the basis there is likely to be at least one student in the classroom with an unseen disability. This means providing advance copies of teaching materials via a managed learning environment, facing students when speaking (this will help partially deaf students who rely on lip reading), writing clearly on the board (or if handwriting is illegible, using a PC and projector in the room to type on an enlarged Word document), using pastel backgrounds for PowerPoint Slides and so on to help those with visual impairments (particularly those with photosensitive epilepsy).

Student E's refusal to write on the board may have less to do with shyness and everything to do with an undeclared learning disability such as dyslexia or other neurodiversity. It is important that in group activities where students are asked to feedback by writing on the board that each group has a student who has volunteered to be a scribe rather than having this role imposed upon them.

9.9.2 Noticing Body Language

Whilst a tutor can notice many things from active listening (the interpretation of verbal and non-verbal messages from students) body language is especially important. This can help to identify the shy student, the bored student, the confused student and the uncomfortable or distressed student. Verbal communication can also help to reveal language barriers both in terms of English as a second language but also unfamiliarity with jargon or colloquialism or even formal language used by a tutor. A tutor should be able to communicate with ease with all students regardless of whether they are international students or

---

[37] Michael Barber, *Gravity Assist: Propelling Higher Education Towards a Brighter Future. Report of the Digital Teaching and Learning Review* (Office for Students, 2021).

come from a national region that is different to that of the tutor. A tutor should not allow accents to be a bar to communication and should not equate accents with poor communication skills, particularly when setting assessments involving oral presentations. Noticing difference should also include celebrating difference.

9.9.3 Noticing as an Aid to Change

Noticing also impacts on the professionalism of teaching because it enables a tutor to take what they see in the classroom into the areas of strategy and priority for the institution, as well as forming collaborative relationships with other tutors and support networks. Mason[38] argues that noticing impacts professional development by becoming a source of 'disturbance'. Mason uses disturbance to mean initiating change. Classroom noticing helps with closing the information loop. By acting and reflecting on observations within the classroom, personal tutors may start their own enquiries about what might benefit student wellbeing generally.[39] For example, would students benefit from more flexible modes of delivery because the institution has a large percentage of commuting students or mature students with family responsibilities, or an increased number of late arrival students coming from international destinations? Does the institution's student demographic mean students increasingly have financial worries or competing interests that impact on their studies and wellbeing? If so, should the institution be investing more in support services to ensure student issues can be escalated to the correct support networks across the institution. Interrogating data on attendance rates, referrals to support networks such as wellbeing teams and disability and dyslexia services also helps to close the loop to ensure 'disturbance.' In the classroom the tutor can take an observational role and in this way act as the institution's 'eyes and ears for change' and then feed those observations into the change mechanisms across the university. This might occur for example, by the tutor making suggestions at departmental boards or institutional committee meetings about steps that could help the student experience, engagement and attainment based on observations made in the classroom.

Noticing also impacts on professional development in the identification of areas of priority for research and scholarship in the field of teaching and learning to allow the tutor to develop their scholarship based on their interactions with their students.

---

[38] Mason (n 34) 139.
[39] See also Chapter 11.

9.10 CONCLUSION

You will inevitably come across situations inside and outside of the classroom which cause you to become concerned about student wellbeing. This is part and parcel of the job. You should not feel alone in facing those situations and should always seek assistance and support from other more experienced colleagues when appropriate. Nonetheless, it is important to equip yourself with the tools needed to identify and deal with student wellbeing issues. In this chapter we have focused on three things you can incorporate into your classroom practice (whether online or in-person) which will help you respond to student wellbeing issues: confidentiality, inclusivity, and noticing. As a result, remembering the following when dealing with students will help:

- Student disclosures require us to consider whether we can mitigate the impact of factors affecting student classroom participation. Therefore, consider what adjustments we need to make to facilitate their engagement, and how we might take these changes forward.
- Ensuring our classrooms and practices are inclusive assists in facilitating student learning and allows us to draw on their diverse experiences. It also encourages students to build positive staff-student and peer relationships that are essential in creating a sense of community and belonging and promoting positive student wellbeing.
- Building relationships will assist us in 'noticing' when students may need support and provides an opportunity for us to celebrate difference.
- When we actively listen to, observe, and reflect on the experiences we share with our students in the classroom, this also provides a means for us to promote change not only in our own practice, but more widely.

10. Integrating wellbeing into the law school curriculum

Emma Jones

Some words appear to have a natural synergy, such as 'eggs' and 'bacon', 'cat' and 'mouse' or (for tort lawyers, at least) 'snail' and 'ginger beer.' Others appear more disparate, or even contradictory, in nature. The terms 'law' and 'wellbeing' would traditionally be placed squarely within the latter category. Law has often been perceived and portrayed as focused upon legal rights and responsibilities, on remedies and redress (often, within private law, financial in nature) and on rules and regulations. It prizes a particular form of reason and rationality which it views as objective, neutral and emotionless.[1] In contrast, wellbeing has developed as a ubiquitous, but also rather nebulous term, perhaps belonging in the realm of yoga, appealing sunsets and tranquil shorelines, but certainly not within law.

Indeed, the term 'wellbeing' can be defined in a range of different ways.[2] However, for the purposes of this chapter, I have adopted the definition given by the World Health Organisation which sees mental health as 'a state of well-being in which an individual realizes his or her own abilities, can cope with the normal stresses of life, can work productively and is able to make a contribution to his or her community.[3] As Baron puts it, it is about ensuring law students are not just 'surviving' but also 'thriving'.[4] I am also taking what is termed a dual continuum view, namely, acknowledging that a student could have a diagnosed mental illness, but have high levels of wellbeing through managing it in appropriate ways. On the other hand, a student with no diag-

---

[1] Colin James, 'Seeing things as we are. Emotional intelligence and clinical legal education' (2005) 8 International Journal of Clinical Legal Education 123.
[2] Rachel Dodge, Annette P. Daly, Jan Huyton, and Lalage D. Sanders, 'The challenge of defining wellbeing' (2012) 2(3) International Journal of Wellbeing 222.
[3] World Health Organisation, Health and Well-Being (2022), available at: who.int/data/gho/data/major-themes/health-and-well-being (accessed 3 October 2023).
[4] Paula Baron, 'Thriving in the Legal Academy' (2008) 17(1&2) Legal Education Review 27.

nosed mental illness could have low levels of wellbeing as a result of their individual circumstances and specific life events that have arisen.[5]

In recent times, there has been a definite shift towards reconciling the terms 'law' and 'wellbeing' and the concepts and values they represent. For example, via feminist and critical legal thought,[6] the development of the 'law and emotions' movement,[7] and the growing interest in therapeutic jurisprudence, a heuristic which argues for the importance of acknowledging and evaluating the ways in which the law and its actors' impact upon wellbeing.[8] As someone who is entering, or has recently entered, legal academia, it is therefore increasingly likely that you will use the two words in conjunction.

In fact, the growing general interest in wellbeing and law has been mirrored within legal education, with a range of studies exploring law student wellbeing.[9] To say this is wholly recent would be misleading. For example, there has been an interest in the US since the mid twentieth century.[10] However, several factors have magnified attention on this area in contemporary times. One of these is the increasing focus on wellbeing within higher education overall (as illustrated by the recent Advance HE Education for Mental Health Toolkit).[11] As student cohorts have diversified, it has been identified that there are increasing numbers of university students both formally disclosing and more informally self-reporting mental health issues and difficulties with poor wellbeing.[12] This is likely to have been exacerbated by the challenges created

---

[5] Universities UK, *Stepchange: Mentally Healthy Universities* (2020) 8, available at: universitiesuk.ac.uk/sites/default/files/field/downloads/2021-07/uuk-stepchange-mhu.pdf#page=12 (accessed 3 October 2023).

[6] Joanne Conaghan, *Law and Gender* (Oxford University Press, 2013).

[7] Susan A. Bandes (ed), *The Passions of Law* (New York University Press, 2000).

[8] David C. Yamada, 'Therapeutic Jurisprudence: Foundations, Expansion, and Assessment' (2020) 75 University of Miami Law Review 660.

[9] Kenneth S. Sheldon and Larry S. Krieger, 'Understanding the Negative Effects of Legal Education on Law Students: A Longitudinal Study of Self-Determination Theory' (2007) 33 Personality and Social Psychology Bulletin 883; Norm Kelk and others, *Courting the Blues: Attitudes Towards Depression in Australian Law Students and Lawyers* (Brain & Mind Research Institute, 2009).

[10] Cf. Andrew S. Watson, 'Teaching mental health concepts in the law school' (1963) 33(1) American Journal of Orthopsychiatry 115.

[11] Advance HE, *Education for Mental Health Toolkit* (2022), available at: advance-he.ac.uk/teaching-and-learning/curricula-development/education-mental-health-toolkit (accessed 3 October 2023).

[12] Randstad, *A Degree of Uncertainty. Students Wellbeing in Higher Education* (2020), available at: randstad.co.uk/employers/areas-of-expertise/student-support/student-mental-health-report-2020/ (accessed 3 October 2023).

during the Covid-19 global pandemic.[13] Such increases have led to a greater focus upon wellbeing by bodies such as the Office for Students, as well as individual institutions.[14] It has also led to a developing focus on a 'whole university' approach to wellbeing.[15] This includes a consideration of all aspects of the student experience, including learning and teaching.[16] It also implies that everyone, including early career academics, has a part to play in promoting positive student wellbeing.

Another key factor is the increasing discipline-specific data suggesting students' wellbeing deteriorates during their time studying law.[17] Although the data on this is not conclusive, there have been a number of studies in other jurisdictions, particularly the US and Australia, which suggest there are discipline-specific factors which negatively impact upon student wellbeing, such as the levels of academic demands and the intense competition for legal careers.[18] The focus on 'thinking like a lawyer' with its rigid emphasis on a (perceived) rational and non-emotive way of thinking has also been identified as problematic, detaching students from intuitive ways of thinking and disconnecting them from healthy emotional responses and reactions.[19] Within the UK, the data is insufficiently developed to reach such a conclusion, but there are early indications this is potentially the case.[20] If we want law students to

---

[13] Nicola Frampton and Dom Smithies, *University Mental Health: Life in a Pandemic. Listening to higher education communities throughout 2020/2021*, available at: studentminds.org.uk/lifeinapandemic.html (accessed 3 October 2023).

[14] Office for Students, *Student Wellbeing and Protection*, available at: officeforstudents .org .uk/ advice -and -guidance/ student -wellbeing -and -protection/ (accessed 3 October 2023).

[15] See above n5; Gareth Hughes and Leigh Spanner, *The University Mental Health Charter* (2019) Student Minds, available at: studentminds.org.uk/charter.html (accessed 3 October 2023).

[16] Ann-Marie Haughton and Jill Anderson, *Embedding Mental Wellbeing in the Curriculum: Maximising Success in Higher Education* (2017) Higher Education Academy, available at: advance-he.ac.uk/knowledge-hub/embedding-mental-wellbeing -curriculum-maximising-success-higher-education (accessed 3 October 2023).

[17] See above n 9.

[18] Natalie K. Skead and Shane L. Rogers, 'Do Law Students Stand Apart from Other University Students in Their Quest for Mental Health: A Comparative Study on Wellbeing and Associated Behaviours in Law and Psychology Students' (2015) 42–43 International Journal of Law and Psychiatry 81; Rachael Field, James Duffy and Colin James (eds), *Promoting Law Student and Lawyer Well-Being in Australia and Beyond* (Routledge, 2016).

[19] Colin James, 'Lawyers' wellbeing and professional legal education' (2008) 42(1) The Law Teacher 85.

[20] Emma Jones, Rajvinder Samra and Mathijs Lucassen 'The world at their fingertips? The mental wellbeing of online distance-based law students' (2019) 53(1) The Law Teacher 49.

flourish and thrive, we therefore need to explicitly consider whether and how our teaching design and delivery is impacting our students' wellbeing.

10.1 UNDERSTANDING THE IMPORTANCE OF WELLBEING WITHIN THE CURRICULUM

Within university settings, wellbeing has often been characterised as a pastoral issue, often separated wholly or in part from academic studies.[21] This is perhaps understandable when those most involved in such studies, namely academics, may feel ill-equipped to support student wellbeing. As an individual entering the legal academy, you may have found you were provided with training and support to develop your expertise within research and teaching. It is unlikely you will have received similar support for pastoral work and you may well feel a sense of 'imposter syndrome' in dealing with issues often characterised as non-academic.[22] The workload demands upon academics and the lack of value traditionally placed upon such tasks ('academic housework'), also militate against appropriate training and support being provided.[23] Instead, most universities will have well-developed central support services designed to take on the majority of this pastoral workload. While such central support services are incredibly important and valuable, there is a strong argument they are not, on their own, sufficient. Increasingly within universities it is becoming clear that academic and pastoral aspects cannot be neatly delineated or separated.

Firstly, there may be a range of issues with students accessing such support services, and the level of provision available. There may be concerns about a perceived stigma around such services and waiting lists before appropriate assistance becomes available. Secondly, it is likely a student will initially be signposted to such support services via someone in an academic role.[24] Drawing upon interviews with 52 academics at five universities within the UK, Hughes et al note that 'Academics described a frontline role, in terms of student wellbeing, as they are more immediately accessible than support services and have pre-existing relationships with their students'.[25] You are

---

[21] Sue Clegg, Sally Bradley and Karen Smith, '"I've had to swallow my pride": help seeking and self-esteem' (2006) 25(2) Higher Education Research & Development 101, 103.
[22] See also Chapter 2.
[23] Thamar Melanie Heijstra, Finnborg Salome Steinthorsdóttir and Thorgerdur Einarsdóttir, 'Academic career making and the double-edged role of academic housework' (2017) 29(6) Gender and Education 764, 764.
[24] See also Chapter 3
[25] Gareth Hughes, Mehr Panjwani, Priya Tulcidas and Dr Nicola Byrom, *Student Mental Health: The Role and Experiences of Academics* (January 2018), p. 5, available at: studentminds.org.uk/uploads/3/7/8/4/3784584/180129_student_mental_health

likely to find you are having to deal with student wellbeing issues, from supporting personal tutees to advising students affected by sensitive content within teaching materials. This means it is important that you prepare yourself psychologically and emotionally by practising good self-care and ensuring you maintain appropriate boundaries and know when to signpost. Many universities offer training on this, and there are also likely to be more senior colleagues who have experience in this work, so it is important you feel able to reach out for training and support.

Dealing with student wellbeing issues is now an inescapable (if under-acknowledged) part of the academic role. Of course, it can be argued (with some justification) that this is a wider issue around the need for additional resourcing of central support services and for institutional mechanisms to allow interventions at an earlier stage. However, there are also compelling positive reasons why academics should engage with student wellbeing, not least the benefits it brings students in terms of their sense of belonging and community.[26] Some such reasons relate to the personal fulfilment and satisfaction such work can bring. However, other reasons relate specifically to the need to provide high quality teaching within universities. There is a bi-directional relationship between students' wellbeing and their studies. A student's wellbeing will affect aspects of their learning, including their motivation, depth of engagement and ability to focus.[27] Conversely, the design and delivery of teaching will affect a student's wellbeing, from the stress and anxiety that can be generated by traditional examinations to the pleasure and sense of achievement in grasping a complex legal concept.[28] Therefore, each time an academic is involved in teaching and learning activities they are involved in activities which will directly impact upon student wellbeing and which are directly impacted by student wellbeing. Applying this specifically to legal academics and law schools, it means that what is included within a curriculum, how it is designed and how it is delivered acts as a key intersection between the two. Put simply, the law school curriculum is key to law student wellbeing.

_the_role_and_experience_of_academics__student_minds_pdf.pdf (accessed 3 October 2023).

[26] See also Chapter 4.

[27] Thomas Kötter, Josefin Wagner, Linda Brüheim and Edgar Voltmer, 'Perceived medical school stress of undergraduate medical students predicts academic performance: an observational study' (2017) 17(1) BMC Medical Education 1; Michaela C. Pascoe, Sarah E. Hetrick and Alexandra G. Parker, 'The impact of stress on students in secondary school and higher education' (2020) 25(1) International Journal of Adolescence and Youth 104.

[28] See above n 16; Mohammad Mofatteh, 'Risk factors associated with stress, anxiety, and depression among university undergraduate students' (2020) 8(1) AIMS Public Health 36; Jan McArthur, *Assessment for Social Justice* (Bloomsbury, 2018).

Of course, it may be that an academic chooses not to consider the role of wellbeing within teaching and learning. Adapting the arguments of Fish in relation to values, they may argue it is outside of their role and expertise, or it would involve them in some way becoming a 'counsellor' or 'therapist'.[29] More cynically, it may be they are choosing to prioritise research, do not see it as helpful for promotion, or simply feel there are other people who should shoulder the load. It may be that you also choose not to engage with the role of wellbeing within teaching and learning. If so, it is important to be aware that such a decision is not neutral. In fact, ignoring potential implications for wellbeing within teaching design and delivery will, in itself, have repercussions for wellbeing. For example, teaching a sensitive topic without providing a content warning could generate distress amongst some students. Perhaps some academics would argue that, by teaching within the general parameters set by the relevant institution or law school, they are able to assume wellbeing issues have already been sufficiently acknowledged. Unfortunately, the data around student wellbeing highlighted towards the start of this chapter suggests this is simply not the case.

10.2 WAYS TO INTEGRATE WELLBEING INTO THE CURRICULUM

If it is accepted that wellbeing and teaching and learning are inter-connected, the next step is to consider how wellbeing can be acknowledged and incorporated into the curriculum in ways which promote both positive wellbeing and positive outcomes for learning and teaching. Not just as part of a 'one off' skills module or extra-curricular session (although both have some value) but as an integral part of the law degree. This may seem challenging, but there is evidence to suggest that, in fact, the two aims are mutually compatible. Indeed, each aim actively supports the other. Healthy study is usually the most effective, productive and sustainable form of study. For example, revising for short periods with breaks in-between is likely to reduce stress and anxiety whilst at the same time facilitating the absorption of the materials.[30] To achieve such a 'win-win' scenario, there needs to be careful thought over how to integrate wellbeing into the curriculum. This section will focus specifically upon how to do this within individual law school modules, focusing on three ways: content, design and delivery. The strongest form of integration will include all three

---

[29] Stanley Fish, *Save the World on Your Own Time* (Oxford University Press, 2008).
[30] Gareth Hughes, *Be Well, Learn Well. Improve Your Wellbeing and Academic Performance* (MacMillan Education Ltd., 2020).

approaches, although the balance between these is likely to vary significantly depending upon the institutional setting, the overall focus of each individual law programme and the objectives of the module itself.

10.2.1 Curriculum Content

One way you may be able to integrate wellbeing into curriculum content is by including wellbeing-related topics within the module. The content of such topics will vary considerably depending upon the module's focus. For example, if teaching on a module exploring criminal law you may consider including resources examining the impact of the criminal justice system upon the psychological wellbeing of the victim.[31] On a public law module you may instead choose to consider an issue such as the way measures around wellbeing have been framed and implemented within devolved jurisdictions.[32]

Integrating wellbeing into curriculum content can also involve introducing questions around wellbeing to established topics, even where there is not an obvious wellbeing-focus to them. For example, when using case law, you could encourage students to look beyond the facts to the underlying human story involved. This could be by way of asking a simple question ('how do you think this judgment affected the wellbeing of the claimant?', 'do you think that dealing with the facts of this case will have impacted the judge/prosecution or defence lawyers?'). It could involve a more in-depth exploration using methods such as narrative techniques.[33]

The key benefits to both these methods are that they raise the visibility of wellbeing as a legitimate and valuable focus of discussion and exploration, provide students with an appropriate vocabulary to engage in such conversations, and challenge any existing stigma around the acknowledgment of wellbeing as a relevant topic within law. A barrier to their implementation may be the need for you to potentially undertake both content-specific and pedagogic research to determine where and how to incorporate such content. However, it may well be you are already undertaking this process generally in relation to module content. Therefore, it is arguably simply extending the scope of an existing process of content design and review, rather than introducing a cumbersome new burden.

---

[31] See e.g., Jim Parsons and Tiffany Bergin, 'The impact of criminal justice involvement on victims' mental health' (2010) 23(2) Journal of Trauma Stress 182.

[32] See e.g., Jennifer Wallace, *Wellbeing and Devolution. Reframing the Role of Government in Scotland, Wales and Northern Ireland* (Springer Nature, 2019).

[33] Dawn Watkins and Laura Guihen, 'Using Narrative and Metaphor in Formative Feedback' (2018) 68(1) Journal of Legal Education 154 at pp. 155–56.

Another barrier can be an understandable fear that such content may be overly challenging, distressing or in some way 'triggering' for students. Of course, it is important to acknowledge the potential difficulties that can arise when incorporating potentially sensitive content. However, this is not a wellbeing-specific issue in itself. Sensitive content is routinely dealt with in modules such as those on criminal law and/or sexual offences. This is done despite the potential challenges that may arise because such content is viewed as legitimate, and perhaps even core, for the study of law as a discipline. Why are wellbeing-related topics not viewed in the same way? If you are being discouraged from doing this, I would suggest the reasons are more to do with the underlying values and concerns that have (and do) shape legal education rather than there being any necessity for one type of content to be privileged over the other. Treating wellbeing-related content in a similar way to other types of sensitive content can and should be done.

Incorporating wellbeing in this way does not mean ignoring the potential challenges, in fact it is likely to require you to carefully consider issues such as sensitive content warnings.[34] However, it is not necessary for this thought process to be undertaken in isolation. Instead, it can be informed by discussions with your colleagues and the approaches already taken within the law school. It may also be that central university support services with an interest in wellbeing are able to contribute. For example, at the University of Sheffield I worked with the Student Wellbeing Service to produce a video and accompanying guidance on dealing with sensitive material for law and criminology students.

Overall, there are a range of ways you can incorporate wellbeing into the content of module curriculum. Although the specifics may be module-dependent, you can incorporate relevant preparation into your general work on content and draw upon the existing knowledge that exists around potentially sensitive content.

10.2.2 Curriculum Design

The second way you may be able to integrate wellbeing into the curriculum is via the design of the module. It is likely that module design will, in part, be dictated by departmental or institutional preference, for example, in relation to the number of weeks in a semester, the routine hours scheduled for teaching, and the size and number of classrooms available. However, a module team will

---

[34] For a valuable discussion in the US context see Francesca Laguardia, Venezia Michalsen and Holly Rider-Milkovich, 'Trigger warnings' (2017) 66(4) Journal of Legal Education 882.

potentially have the flexibility to make some decisions, such as the division of teaching hours between small and larger group sessions, the format of the sessions, and the timing across the module. Therefore, there are likely to be opportunities for you to contribute suggestions and ideas whether through module team meetings, or wider curriculum review processes.

Module design impacts upon wellbeing in a huge variety of ways. One way relates to the format of teaching used. A traditional division within legal education is between large scale lectures and smaller group seminars or tutorials.[35] Each of these can have different wellbeing implications. For example, a student who is experiencing low wellbeing levels could find a lecture, where they can simply be a face in the crowd, less intimidating to attend. However, they may also feel unable to ask questions, or to contribute to consolidate their knowledge, in such a setting. Therefore, careful thought needs to be given to the appropriate balance to be struck.

As legal education evolves, a wider range of formats of teaching are increasingly being included, particularly within smaller group settings (for example, different types of group work and peer learning).[36] While these have many pedagogic benefits, they can also challenge students' wellbeing in different ways. For example, a student who finds larger groups overwhelming or isolating may appreciate the relational aspects of group work. However, conversely, they may find balancing the demands and expectations of group members with the need to prioritise their own wellbeing difficult and distressing.

One format which has evolved within legal education is that of Problem-Based Learning ('PBL'), where students work in groups to address a complex issue with no pre-determined 'right answer', potentially mirroring the approach of a legal professional when meeting a client for the first time.[37] The wellbeing implications of this approach seem rather under-explored, but it can be speculated that such work could foster a sense of competency and relatedness where students are able to learn in an active and engaged manner (both attributes related to heightened wellbeing).[38] At the same time, the tensions that can arise within group dynamics and the unfamiliarity and uncertainty where the

---

[35] Alison Bone, 'The twenty-first century law student' (2009) 43(3) The Law Teacher 222.

[36] Philippa Ryan, 'Teaching collaborative problem-solving skills to law students' (2017) 51(2) The Law Teacher 138.

[37] Heloísa Oliveira, Tatiana Sanches and João Martins, 'Problem-based learning in a flipped classroom: a case study for active learning in legal education in international law' (2022) The Law Teacher, https://www.tandfonline.com/doi/full/10.1080/03069400.2022.2040934 (accessed 14 December 2023).

[38] Richard M. Ryan and Edward L. Deci, 'Self-determination theory and the facilitation of intrinsic motivation, social development, and well-being' (2000) 55(1) American Psychologist 68.

process and outcome are open-ended also have the potential to undermine these attributes.[39]

These potential benefits and challenges mean that if you were seeking to include PBL within a module you would need to carefully consider how to alleviate potential issues and enhance the possible benefits to wellbeing. This could include beginning by providing detailed instructional materials both in writing and verbally (for example, listing expectations and time scales). Other techniques could involve providing a worked example/case study of the approach; an initial small-scale 'practice run' of the approach; building in regular 'check-in' points with individual groups/students; explicitly incorporating reflective elements requiring exploration of the challenges involved in PBL and using formative assessments to build student confidence in their understanding of, and approach to PBL.

Another way in which module design impacts upon wellbeing arises when considering assessment types. For example, an in-person examination (a traditional staple within law) may generate stress as students worry about the need to memorise key legislation and cases and the time pressures involved. At the same time, students tackling coursework may find issues with motivation and procrastination. More novel forms of assessment may generate anxiety as students are unsure what to expect and what is expected from them.[40] If you are designing assessments, this complexity requires you to carefully consider wellbeing implications. This could include scaffolding students' exposure to the particular approach being used, including a related formative assessment, allowing for structured reflection on formative feedback, providing a detailed marking rubric, and allowing students the opportunity to 'mark' a sample assessment. Of course, none of these steps solely relate to the integration of wellbeing in the curriculum – they will often form part of general good practice in teaching – but by viewing them through a wellbeing lens it affords an opportunity to ensure the two align and enhance each other.

One objection that may be raised to incorporating wellbeing into curriculum design is that it is intellectually problematic in that it 'removes' the type of rigour, stretch and challenge which is required for academic legal study. A focus upon wellbeing can be characterised as overly paternalistic and disempowering for students, characterising them in a way which diminishes

---

[39] The Advance HE Education for Mental Health Toolkit (n 11) contains helpful resources on this topic.

[40] Emma Jones, Michael Priestley, Liz Brewster, Susan J. Wilbraham, Gareth Hughes and Leigh Spanner, 'Student wellbeing and assessment in higher education: the balancing act' (2021) 46(3) Assessment & Evaluation in Higher Education 438.

their potential.[41] I would argue that much of this critique results from a misunderstanding in the way the notion of wellbeing is being conceptualised, for example, by equating it with self-esteem or 'the means to be happy'.[42] If we view wellbeing as being about flourishing and thriving it is necessary for the curriculum to include the type of rigour, stretch and challenge which encourage students to develop and grow, which allows them to achieve more both intellectually and personally and which imbues academic study with meaning.[43]

The examples of module design which have been discussed demonstrate it is highly unlikely there will be a linear choice to be made between something that is 'good' or 'bad' for wellbeing. Instead, there is considerable complexity in how such issues need to be approached. However, when making curriculum design choices, I would suggest there are two fundamental questions you should ask: Firstly, what are the potential impacts of this decision on student wellbeing? Secondly, how will this be experienced by students who may be undergoing wellbeing issues? This allows a dialogue (whether internal or with module team members and other colleagues) on the specific module's design. Once again, there is likely to be support available both in the law school and wider university to assist you in this process. It is not about attempting to 'reinvent the wheel', but rather about ensuring the values which are prioritised during module design include its relationship with student wellbeing.

10.2.3 Curriculum Delivery

The third way you may be able to integrate wellbeing into the curriculum is via the delivery of the module. Delivery can incorporate some of the aspects discussed above in relation to 'design' (such as the format of sessions).[44] However, the aspect I particularly want to focus upon here is the way you tackle the delivery of any sessions you are assigned on specific modules, with a brief additional nod to the types of academic support you may offer outside of timetabled teaching sessions.

With regard to the former, within any law school it is likely that there will be a diverse range of teaching styles. Your own teaching style may be influenced by any training received (or lack thereof), pedagogic preferences and your own educational experiences. It is also likely to develop over time, as you gain further experience. In addition, workload demands, personal preferences and

---

[41] Kathryn Ecclestone and Dennis Hayes, *The Dangerous Rise of Therapeutic Education* (Routledge, 2009).
[42] Ibid at p. ix.
[43] Caroline Strevens and Rachael Field (eds), *Educating for Well-Being in Law: Positive Professional Identities and Practice* (Routledge, 2019).
[44] See also Chapter 9.

other external factors may have a part to play, for example, a lack of time to prepare for a session could lead to a more didactic, transmissional approach being taken.[45] Regardless of the drivers for specific teaching styles, the way they are experienced by students is likely to impact upon their wellbeing.

Perhaps one of the most extreme examples of this within legal education is the use of the Socratic method. Commonly associated with law teaching in the US, although variants persist elsewhere, it consists of a series of questions from a teacher to a student. The student will initially be required to set out their position, and then to justify it as the teacher identifies potential weaknesses in the argument put forward.[46] This method has increasingly been critiqued for its impacts on wellbeing. For example, Spencer argues it prizes the contributions of those students with the confidence and cultural capital to verbally contribute within teaching settings at the expense of those with quieter, more reflective approaches to learning and those who may feel unwilling or unable to contribute. It therefore contributes to the adversarialism of common law systems and disregards the potential for less aggressive alternatives.[47] My personal preference is to avoid this technique, precisely because of the potentially detrimental impacts upon wellbeing. If you do want or need to engage in it, I would suggest carefully considering how you can ameliorate these, for example, by asking for volunteers and not putting any individual student 'on the spot,' and by managing student expectations through clearly setting out the approach taken in module materials.

Whilst some teaching styles may be actively harmful to wellbeing, it is also possible to identify practices and techniques that can enhance wellbeing. For example, Bromberger refers to 'the nurturing teacher' who fosters a teaching setting most conducive to learning by acknowledging, understanding and working with the emotions present within the classroom.[48] Acting in nurturing ways could include displaying interest and enthusiasm for a topic, considering your body language and tone of voice and thinking carefully about how you and your students interact with the physical space. For example, sitting behind a desk could be viewed as a 'barrier' to engagement, mimicking a (potentially intimidating) schoolroom environment.

---

[45] Siobhan Wray and Gail Kinman, 'The psychosocial hazards of academic work: an analysis of trends' (2022) 47(4) Studies in Higher Education 771.
[46] Matt Hlinak, 'The socratic method 2.0' (2014) 31 Journal of Legal Studies Education 1.
[47] Rachel Spencer, 'Hell is other people': rethinking the Socratic method for quiet law students' (2022) 56(1) The Law Teacher 90.
[48] Nikki Bromberger, 'Enhancing law student learning – the nurturing teacher' (2010) 20(1/2) Legal Education Review 45, 51.

In reference to academic support outside of the lecture or seminar room, there are also nurturing approaches that can be taken.[49] Some such approaches may include sending regular emails or messages to cohorts of students reminding them of relevant events and deadlines and the support available, putting a sign on your office door indicating your availability to speak to students and the best means to contact you, and adding your photograph to your module's Virtual Learning Environment.

As discussed in relation to module design, much of this is good pedagogic practice in any event. However, it should be acknowledged any adjustments to teaching style may require additional time and effort on the part of the individual legal academic who is reflecting upon what changes should be made, and how to implement them. It is vital that the wellbeing of legal academics is also acknowledged, and that excessive and inappropriate demands are not placed upon them.[50] Therefore, there should be an expectation that the wider law school will provide programme level approaches, appropriate resources and support to facilitate anything above the type of iterative development and adjustment that is a necessary part of all teaching practice. If these resources and support are not given to you, it should not be that you feel compelled to prioritise student wellbeing over your own. Make such adjustments as and when you can, but recognise the limits to what any one legal academic can achieve if they are not in a supportive environment.

10.3 TEACHING CONTRACT LAW: A CASE STUDY

To explore the integration of wellbeing into a module in a practical sense, I have chosen to focus upon the ways in which wellbeing can be integrated into a module on contract law. One of the reasons I have chosen this is the fact I teach contract law, and have done for some time, so it has a particular resonance for me. However, there are other reasons which make it a suitable candidate. Firstly, it has traditionally (within law of obligations) been seen as one of the foundational subjects for law.[51] Secondly, it perhaps has less obvious links

---

[49] See also Chapter 11.

[50] Liz Brewster, Emma Jones, Michael Priestley, Susan J. Wilbraham, Leigh Spanner and Gareth Hughes, 'Look after the staff and they would look after the students' cultures of wellbeing and mental health in the university setting' (2022) 46(4) Journal of Further and Higher Education 548.

[51] Legal Education and Training Review, *Setting Standards: The future of legal services education and training regulation in England and Wales* Annex 1, available at: legalservicesboard.org.uk/our-work/work-related-to-previous-years/education-and-training/education-and-training-legal-education-and-training-review (accessed 3 October 2023).

with wellbeing than a topic such as criminal law, public law or even tort law, hopefully demonstrating that wellbeing can be integrated into any law module.

In terms of wellbeing and module content, one way in which wellbeing can be incorporated is within the discussions of the tensions that exist in contract law between traditional notions of freedom of contract and the increasing focus upon consumer protection.[52] The potential vulnerability of consumers has not just financial consequences, but also implications for the financial and psychological wellbeing of the individuals involved. At a more theoretical level, relational contract theory could also provide an interesting opening for exploring the role of values and relationships within contract formation, and their links to the wellbeing of both individuals and businesses.[53] There is also some interesting work on contract law and emotions which could be drawn upon to open-up wellbeing-related dialogue, such as Stannard's discussion of undue influence and emotions.[54]

Wellbeing could also be highlighted within other seemingly non-related topics, for example, considering the challenges to wellbeing suffered by Mr Addis as a result of the breach of his employment contract by the Gramophone Company when he was working as their manager in Calcutta.[55] By giving him six months' notice of termination of employment, but then appointing a different manager and preventing Mr Addis from carrying out his duties, it was clear that Mr Addis felt humiliated and undermined. Nevertheless, he was unable to obtain non-pecuniary damages for the pain and suffering stemming from the manner in which he was dismissed. What does that say about the underlying values of contract law? How does more recent case law on non-pecuniary loss for breach of contract suggest these values may be changing, as the exceptions to this general rule are widened?[56]

In terms of module design, my anecdotal sense is that contract law is commonly taught in relatively traditional ways, towards the start of a law degree. Its positioning in this sense is important as it means it can be used to encourage and scaffold learning and other behaviours which are identified as

---

[52] For a recent reframing of this, which emphasises the underlying ethical frameworks, see Chris Willett, 'Re-theorising consumer law' (2018) 77(1) The Cambridge Law Journal 179.

[53] Ian R. Macneil 'Contracts: Adjustment of Long-Term Economic Relations under Classical, Neoclassical, and Relational Contract Law' (1978) 72 Northwestern University Law Review 854.

[54] John Stannard, 'The Emotional Dynamics of Undue Influence' in John Stannard and Heather Conway (eds), The Emotional Dynamics of Law and Legal Discourse (Hart Publishing, 2016) 59–82.

[55] *Addis v Gramphone Co. Ltd.* [1909] AC 488.

[56] *Watts & Anor v Morrow* [1991] 1 WLR 1421 (CA); *Farley v Skinner* [2002] 2 AC 732 (HL).

important to the law degree. For example, it could be that the first session is a more social experience, designed to ease students into university learning environments and develop a sense of community and belonging. More relaxed activities relating contracts to everyday life (buying a coffee, getting on a bus) could be used to scaffold student learning in an engaging way. Different teaching techniques could also be used across the module. Having practised construction law myself, I can see how students could be allocated into groups representing different parties to a dispute, or to trace through the negotiation and formation of a contract for a new shopping centre or leisure centre. Such group work would require careful scaffolding, but could again foster belonging and community.

When considering module delivery, contract law can perhaps be seen as somewhat dry. However, this affords opportunities to encourage students to question their assumptions and begin to see the human interest in the vast range of case law available. Teaching contractual topics with enthusiasm and relating them to everyday life allows students to begin to navigate the complex relationships between law and society within a supportive and open environment. The relative lack of sensitive content in comparison to some other legal topics also allows students to begin to acclimatise to the study of unfamiliar or difficult material in a way which can inculcate healthy approaches for use when more sensitive content is introduced elsewhere.

10.4 INTEGRATING WELLBEING AT A PROGRAMME LEVEL

Much of this chapter has focused on integrating wellbeing in individual modules This is on the assumption that most legal academics will be able to affect some form of meaningful change at this level. However, it is equally (if not more) important that wellbeing is also integrated at a programme level. The discussion above relating to content, design and delivery will still largely apply, but there are several other important aspects that come to the fore at the programme level. Although at the point when you are reading this chapter you may not be in the position to make programme-level changes, these are points to bear in mind for the future. You may also find opportunities arise (for example, via committee memberships or at staff meetings) to offer suggestions around these.

Firstly, the need to collect and analyse data to inform the continued integration of wellbeing. For wellbeing to be incorporated into the curriculum in a sustainable way, it must be done in an evidence-based manner and with in-built processes for evaluating the impacts.[57] Secondly, the notion of assisting students to navigate the transitions that occur throughout the programme. The transitions into, through and out of legal study can have significant impacts upon, and be affected by, student wellbeing.[58] Thirdly, it is important to think about skills development at a programme level. This includes academic skills but also wider skills relating to wellbeing, such as self-reflection and emotional literacy.[59]

Taking such an approach at programme level affords a sense of consistency which allows students to form appropriate expectations and understand the boundaries of the law curriculum, allowing them to relax enough to explore within those in a healthy and appropriate manner.

10.5 A WELLBEING CHECKLIST

This brief checklist is designed to consolidate some of the key points raised above. It may serve as a helpful starting point for developing specific module or programme level checklists within law schools.

10.5.1 Initial Considerations

- What data relating to student wellbeing and teaching and learning currently exists at an institutional, law school, programme and module level.

10.5.2 Module Content

- What wellbeing-related topics can be included?
- How can other topics incorporate discussions of wellbeing?

10.5.3 Module Design

- What are the potential impacts of this decision on student wellbeing?
- How will this be experienced by students who may be undergoing wellbeing issues?

---

[57] A useful website covering these issues is https://www.whatworkswellbeing.org (accessed 3 October 2023).
[58] Eilidh Cage, Emma Jones, Gemma Ryan, Gareth Hughes and Leigh Spanner, 'Student mental health and transitions into, through and out of university: student and staff perspectives' (2021) 45(8) Journal of Further and Higher Education 1076.
[59] See above n 18.

10.5.4 Module Delivery

- Are any aspects of delivery potentially detrimental to student wellbeing?
- Are there ways in which student wellbeing could be nurtured through teaching and/or academic support?

10.5.5 Programme-level

- Have student transitions been acknowledged?
- Have skills been scaffolded appropriately?

10.6 CONCLUSION

To take a 'whole law school' approach to wellbeing it is necessary to integrate wellbeing into the legal curriculum. This can be done in a range of ways at both module and programme level. In effect, wellbeing has to become part of the normal everyday business of the law school – something that is routinely acknowledged and explored whenever strategic, pedagogic and other decisions and choices are being made. For legal academics, particularly towards the start of your journey, this can sometimes seem a complex, daunting and time-consuming process. However, there is wider support and knowledge within both law schools and universities that can facilitate such an approach. If we want our students to thrive and flourish it is vital that we take an intentional approach to learning and teaching which values and prioritises wellbeing.

11. Being a personal tutor in a diverse HE sector

Vicky Martin

11.1 THE CHANGING STUDENT COHORT

It is now almost universally accepted that personal tutoring has a huge impact on the student experience.[1] The student–personal tutor relationship can help students feel part of the learning community and connected to the university. The evolution from pupil to student can be highly stressful and a good student–personal tutor relationship can be crucial to ensure that transition is smooth and successful.[2] This may be even more critical for a student who is 'atypical', for example a mature student, one with additional learning requirements, or someone who has taken a non-traditional route to becoming a university student, such as by taking BTEC qualifications rather than A levels, or entering via an access or foundation course. The HE sector has expanded and diversified,[3] meaning we now have a broader spectrum of students entering higher education, with a more varied set of issues and needs.[4] We, as personal tutors, need to expand our horizons to meet these new challenges and provide a proper service to all students.

Students have multiple identities; they are also possibly workers, parents, carers, siblings, and a whole array of other things as well. As such, we need to think about our tutees and their support needs holistically, to ensure all needs are recognised, validated, and met. If we only look at academic issues, we may not be providing the appropriate provision for all our students. By focusing on a single issue, we may even be excluding some students due to their life experi-

---

[1] Kathrine J. McFarlane, 'Tutoring the Tutors: Supporting Effective Personal Tutoring' (2016) 17(1) Active Learning in Higher Education.
[2] Annabel T. Yale, 'The Personal Tutor–Student Relationship: Student Expectations and Experiences of Personal Tutoring in Higher Education' (2019) 43 Journal of Further and Higher Education 533–44.
[3] Dave Lochtie, *Effective Personal Tutoring in Higher Education* (Critical Publishing, 2018).
[4] Yale (n 2).

ences. All students, but particularly those from underrepresented groups, need to feel they belong to their university and programme.[5] As personal tutors we can support this by ensuring the provision we offer to students is supportive, inclusive, and collaborative, and a meaningful and productive experience.

It is also important for students to understand they have many skills they bring to their studies; this is also important if they move into the legal workplace as many employers are now looking for a well-rounded or 'O shaped' lawyer,[6] with soft skills such as 'communication, empathy, courage' and the ability to collaborate.[7] We need to ensure all our students with their very different experiences and cultural capital[8] have the opportunity to acquire these attributes and are guided as to how they can do so. Successful personal tutoring should draw upon the students' unique qualities and validate those lived experiences to empower and assist students to resolve issues they face in university and beyond. The role of the personal tutor is to effectively support students, whatever issues they may be facing; it requires a collaborative approach to problem solving and goal setting. An agreement can then be reached as to areas to focus on to ensure students reach their own personal potential and for their own wellbeing.

In writing the case studies that follow, I have drawn upon my experiences in my current role and in my previous lives as both a criminal defence lawyer and a probation service officer. I hope you find some of the suggestions helpful and that you can implement some of the good practice. One thing to remember is tutors, like students, are all different; we have our own unique set of skills and lived experiences, and this is what makes us great tutors. Don't try to be someone else; bring your authentic self to your meetings with your students.[9] Remember the tips here are only for guidance and sometimes you just need someone else to tell you you're doing a good job to give you the confidence to do a great one. I hope this chapter will validate your views and inspire you to inspire your students.

---

[5] You will see this theme of belonging throughout this book, but in particular in Chapter 4, Chapter 9 and Chapter 10.
[6] See oshaped.com/the-o-shaped-story (accessed 3 October 2023).
[7] See oshaped.com/news/us5sdww8od79ccslt0vznib6tggiso?ss_source=sscampaigns&ss_email_id=61adf5dbb62dc37d368985a9 (accessed 3 October 2023).
[8] Pierre Bourdieu, 'The Forms of Capital' in Imre Szeman and Timothy Kaposy (eds), *Cultural Theory: An Anthology* (Blackwell, 2011).
[9] See also Chapter 2.

11.2　BEING INCLUSIVE AS A PERSONAL TUTOR

Regardless of what the 'job description' entails, what is required to be an effective personal tutor is the ability to build a rapport and trust[10] with our students so we can offer the support they need, whether this is in relation to academic skills, wellbeing, career, or general support and guidance. The job of a personal tutor is not well defined, but Stork and Walker,[11] and Lochtie,[12] have described personal tutors as offering academic support and nurturing wellbeing, as well as referring to expert support. Others state the role is to help students 'manage their own learning and future aspirations.'[13] What is important is that you know how it operates at your university and are aware of the policies and support in place.

In general, there are several key functions which a personal tutor will perform, sometimes with the assistance of other staff (such as student experience tutors). These roles can be grouped into academic support, wellbeing support, active referral, problem solving and career goal setting.

What areas you focus on with individual tutees will be dependent upon several factors, including any issues the student has and what area you have both agreed to concentrate upon. In addition, personal tutors tend to be the face of the university and the first point of contact in relation to general information regarding the institution, school, and programme. We are also there to inspire students and help them reach their full potential through positive interactions. This is a substantial role, which will have a profound impact on the student journey, and potentially be the site of some of the most important interactions you will have with students. In fact, Yale found that a negative experience of the personal tutor experience could have a negative impact on the entirety of the student experience.[14] To be able to assist our tutees, we need to know what areas they want and will accept assistance in, and this could be different for each student. We need to facilitate students to recognise and authenticate their prior experiences.[15]

---

[10]　See also Chapter 3.

[11]　Andrew Storke and Ben Walker, *Becoming an Outstanding Personal Tutor: Supporting Learners through Personal Tutoring and Coaching* (Critical Publishing, 2015).

[12]　Lochtie (n 3).

[13]　Claire Holland, Caroline Westwood and Naveen Hanif, 'Underestimating the Relationship Between Academic Advising and Attainment: A Case Study in Practice' (2020) 5 Frontiers in Educ.

[14]　Yale (n 2).

[15]　Nick Cartwright '"Why is it my problem if they don't take part?" The (non) role of white academics in decolonising the law school' (2020) 54(4) The Law Teacher 532–46.

11.3 EXAMPLES OF GOOD PRACTICE AND RESOURCES THAT HAVE WORKED

Many students, from all backgrounds, find speaking to their tutors intimidating; this appears to be even more true post COVID-19 lockdowns. This may be an even bigger issue for some of our students who have lived through trauma; have been involved with the state due to having looked after status, or through being involved with the criminal justice system; and those students who are arriving with (often undiagnosed) complex mental health issues.

There are three key principles in my personal tutoring strategy:

- Active listening
- Active referral
- Good communication

Active listening is key to ensuring our tutees are properly heard and feel safe to disclose issues that may be concerning them. Active listening is the process of really listening and paying attention while someone else speaks; summarising and reflecting what is said; and withholding judgement and advice. This practice enables the other person to feel heard, validated, and valued. Your tutee may come to speak to you about an assessment grade but on closer listening and discussion, what is really concerning them is not fitting in, feeling overwhelmed or issues outside university that are impacting on their ability to prepare and perform well.

Active referral simply means referring students to the correct person for specialist advice and then actively following this up with the student, the department, or both. As a personal tutor you need to be aware of the central support your institution offers and how your tutees can access it.[16] One of your key duties is to ensure you have at least offered access to the appropriate support services, even if you student does not then go, and to have done so both verbally and in writing.

11.4 GOOD PRACTICE WHEN DEALING WITH STUDENTS WHO ARE OR HAVE BEEN INVOLVED WITH LOCAL AUTHORITIES/ OTHER SERVICES

Tutors can make themselves more approachable and less intimidating by some very simple things such as not sitting behind a desk when speaking with

---

[16] This is a key theme that permeates throughout this book, but see in particular Chapter 2, Chapter 5, Chapter 6 and Chapter 7.

a tutee, to meeting tutees in the university café or other neutral space. Never underestimate how stepping into an office or speaking to someone 'in authority' can make someone feel if they have had previous unpleasant experiences of authority.

11.4.1 Case Study

One student came to my attention due to non-engagement with personal tutoring and the programme generally. They had already had a warning from the university regarding possible withdrawal from the course and responded to my email only due to this warning. They were sporadic in returning emails but eventually I managed to arrange to speak to them online. I am not a fan of online interaction, but for some of our less confident and more anxious students this has become the only way they feel comfortable communicating. You may also encounter similar students who have been involved with their local authority or other organisations and feel let down by them. This student felt they had to prove their worth and struggled with deadlines and rules, but their main issue was not feeling able to come and speak to me in the office and not feeling comfortable on campus.

This student had had such a bad experience of authority that they felt coming onto campus meant they had no control over what happened to them and did not feel able to put themselves in that position. Given that our courses are not online, and attendance is mandatory, this was an obstacle the student needed to overcome. They also needed to realise the warning of withdrawal was not a personal threat aimed at them because of their status, as they saw it, but a regulatory procedure applicable to all students.

This student needed to have information explained to them in entirely unambiguous terms and to be aware of the consequences of not following university regulations, but they also needed support in overcoming their fear of authority and to be able to see that we as tutors wanted to work with them, so they could succeed. This was quite a balancing act, and it was important to be clear about expectations, so I had to have some very direct online conversations with this student about our minimum expectations of them, while also explaining what we could and could not do to assist them. A colleague agreed to meet with this student on campus but outside the offices and teaching rooms in a neutral space. It was important for this student that we as tutors were not on home ground and that they felt at least partly in control, so a neutral space was key.

It is worth remembering that if you feel a conversation is difficult, it will be even more difficult for your student. As much as you can meet on neutral territory you will always have more power in this relationship, and it is important to understand how this might impact on your student, who may become defensive and aggressive. When having difficult conversations, I have found it best to be direct but compassionate and acknowledge what you are saying may not be what the student wants to hear or may make them feel uncomfortable. We should validate their feelings but explain why the conversation is necessary. For example, in this particular case, the student felt we were dismissing their fears and pushing them too much. I had to explain we were having the conversation because we wanted them to succeed; they had made good progress already and we were looking for ways they could progress further. I also explained if we did not care about the student reaching their potential and did not feel that the student was capable of this, we would not suggest it. Often telling the student why you are saying something is enough to make them less uncomfortable. You should not try to avoid issues; students tend to appreciate a direct and honest approach if they understand why the conversation is necessary.

By working with this student and helping them feel more in control by meeting in a neutral space and then making their own decisions about what they needed to do to remain on their learning journey, this student learned the power to succeed was in their own hands and that with the right mindset and determination they could achieve. They also felt able to ask for help with other issues, which at first they did not feel comfortable discussing. In addition, they realised that many of the extra support or sessions available were not just extra work, but a valuable resource to help them develop skills they will need in the future.

11.5 GOOD PRACTICE WHEN DEALING WITH STUDENTS WHO ARE CARERS/PARENTS

At Manchester Met, we have many students who are carers, often unofficially, for other family members, such as a parent, grandparent, or sibling. These students will almost always be commuter students, some may also be mature students. While it is important to remember that each student will be an individual with their own concerns, worries and strengths, those with caring responsibilities will often come to see you with similar issues. The HE system is quite archaic in several ways and can still be geared towards those students whose primary focus is their degree. For example, students are expected to fit any other commitments around their studying; for many carers and parents with e.g., school meetings this will not always be possible. Many parents and carers need practical advice and support about how to navigate the HE systems to allow them to manage their responsibilities and still have an enriching student experience.

Universities will have different policies and practices but key things to assist carers and parents are often linked to negotiating central systems regarding timetabling and attendance. You need to ensure you are aware of the processes in your own institution so you can help students with this. If their timetable does not fit in with school drop off and pick up times, who do they need to liaise with to have their timetable changed and what is the process? If they will be away due to a relative's ill health/hospital appointments etc. what is the process for notifying the university of this absence? These are very practical points that will make a big difference to students with caring responsibilities, it is also important to ensure you know of other institutional support for students with these additional responsibilities. For example, we have a specialist team who look after students who are pregnant in our Disability and Inclusion team. This practical support and advice may be all your students with caring responsibilities require from you.

11.5.1 Case Study

Some carers and parents will have more complex needs depending on the complexity of their own circumstances. For example, a student with physical health issues needed support from our central teams in relation to study skills and assessment extensions. They came to see me as they had failed an assessment and wanted to ensure they could catch up. I was lucky with this student because I had contact with them on the programme, so had built up sufficient trust that they felt able to ask for assistance. Often these students will slip through the gaps unless we seek them out. One of my key points with my tutees is therefore to chase them if they are absent from more than one session: just a quick email saying, 'I noticed you've missed a couple of classes, is everything alright?' can sometimes be sufficient.

This student had missed lessons due to their own ill health but had not been able to catch up due to regular caring responsibilities. They felt they did not deserve any additional support; they simply had to get on with it as best they could. Only by explaining the university had support that was part of their fees did they agree to access this: I was able to help with some subject specific input, but the central study skills team provided assistance and guidance on general assessment skills. The student was also entitled to an extension for other reasons: by bringing this whole support package together, I could facilitate the best possible learning and assessment environment for this student so they could perform at their best. I could only do this because I was aware of all the central support and had the student's trust, so they felt able to speak with me about their issues.

Another student with caring responsibilities had also fallen behind and was struggling to catch up as they felt overwhelmed by their responsibilities. Again, I was fortunate in that I had already built up a relationship with them. They had reached breaking point and sought me out in crisis and in distress. The student had overcome some difficult circumstances to attend university in the first place. They had overcome this earlier adversity, but not dealt with some of the long-term issues it had caused. This student also felt they were not entitled to 'special treatment' and did not want to be a burden. They could not catch up with their studies due to their caring responsibilities, the lack of a quiet place to study at home, and their own health issues.

Fortunately, this student had already accessed wellbeing and counselling support and I encouraged them to make an emergency appointment with their counsellor for specialist help, but I was also able to offer that immediate caring ear, to listen, validate, and offer some practical advice and assistance. I was able to move this student to attend workshops that fitted with their caring arrangements and was able to help them complete the forms for extensions to assessment deadlines, so they had sufficient time to catch up on work they missed due to their own and other's ill health. I also suggested they utilised the university's quiet study space and suggested they speak with our study skills team regarding managing their limited study time. I also kept checking they were keeping their counselling appointments. Further accommodations were required when they sat their assessments, but they did manage to pass the year.

Practical support and an empathetic ear[17] are central to supporting students with additional responsibilities. It is therefore crucial you know what support your institution offers and how students can access this. In addition, many students with caring responsibilities feel they do not need, or do not deserve, any additional support: students should be informed of all available support, but the decision should always be theirs as to what they take up. We may think a particular resource may be helpful, but to someone who is already overtired, overstretched, and overwhelmed it might be an additional chore. We don't always have such a positive outcome immediately, and often it will take several conversations before the time is right for your tutee to access the resources they need. The important thing is to keep reinforcing that these resources are available, and that your tutee is as entitled as any student to make use of these.

11.6 GOOD PRACTICE WHEN DEALING WITH STUDENTS WHO LACK CONFIDENCE AND/OR HAVE IMPOSTER SYNDROME

All students deserve their university place, but many students feel they should not be here, or don't fit in. Imposter syndrome is common among many students, but particularly among high achievers, females, and those from

---

[17] See also Chapters 4 and 9.

underrepresented backgrounds or who are first generation students.[18] Imposter syndrome[19] leaves students feeling they are undeserving of their place on the programme and in fear of being discovered as a fraud.[20] Any student with any lived experience can present with this issue. This may be masked by other concerns, such as a student who is performing well academically being excessively worried about their assessment; students who are capable and well prepared but will not engage in group discussion; or students who simply seem to be disengaging with the programme all together.

11.6.1 Case Study

Two students with very different backgrounds presented with imposter syndrome in different ways and needed different support. One student was a high achiever, the other a first-generation student who was failing: both had progressed beyond first year but believed they were not good enough. One came in search of assistance and feedback, the other was chased due to their non engagement and only attended when they were told they may be withdrawn from the course. Once it was identified that imposter syndrome was the key cause then confidence building was key for both these students, but they were at different levels here. The first-generation student felt they should not be here and would never be accepted; the high achiever sought perfection and felt anything other than a First was a failure.

The first-generation student had deeper rooted confidence issues which required more resources, but also an empathetic ear, to ensure they would continue to work on their confidence rather than simply giving up. Starting with growth mindset tools is useful with a student with very low self-esteem. With this student it was important for them to remember why they had come to university and what their future goal was: students often lose sight of this when struggling with imposter syndrome and other issues. Using vision exercises from the VESPA Mindset Workbook,[21] (a problem solving, self-assessment resource) and confidence building and resilience resources from our central resources, helped the student to see why they were here and what they wanted to achieve. Discussing past successes and their ability to overcome previous concerns helped the student to build resilience.

---

[18] George P. Chrousos and Alexios-Fotios A. Mentis, 'Imposter syndrome threatens diversity' (2005) 367 Science.
[19] See Chapter 2 for a critique of imposter syndrome.
[20] Chrousos and Mentis (n 18).
[21] Steve Oakes and Martin Griffin, *The VESPA Mindset Workbook: 40 activities for FE students that transform commitment, motivation and productivity* (Crown House Publishing, 2019).

This student also benefitted from seeing peers from a similar background succeed and was advised to engage in mentoring schemes. We have several mentoring schemes aimed at different groups of students and the university also runs a 'coffee with a graduate' scheme. These schemes, although primarily aimed at getting students career ready, can also be motivational and inspirational to students. This student did not know anyone within the law and was struggling to see how someone with their background could break into the legal profession. Being introduced to others from a similar background who had succeeded helped to validate the student and enabled them to start participating with the programme again. This was not a straightforward trajectory and there were still times the student felt overwhelmed, but having built up a level of trust and engagement it was easier to monitor and offer support and encouragement.

The high achieving student felt they were not preforming well unless they got a First-class mark in all units: they felt they would not obtain any legal job without those top grades. They came for advice regarding a particular grade. This student needed different resources to the first. They needed feedback on their academic abilities, but they also needed to think about why anything less than a First was not good enough. It was clear there were family expectations of a high-earning job, in part due to the cost of attending university. The student felt they could only do that if they got a First-class degree. It was therefore important to work with the tutee to unpick this belief that the only criteria they will be judged on is academic grades. To do this we used resources from our careers and employability team but also used a skills audit to help them see what else they could bring to an employer and that their overall degree classification did not define them. Using this allowed this student to re-evaluate themselves and see how much they had achieved so far; it also highlighted areas they could work on to increase employability and confidence.

Through using this self-assessment skills audit, this student was able to see they could benefit from getting additional work experience. We looked at pro bono and holiday schemes the student could apply for; the student was able to gain skills and experience they needed and equally importantly grew in confidence from identifying strengths and weaknesses and building up skills.

11.7 GOOD PRACTICE WHEN DEALING WITH STUDENTS WHO HAVE COMPLEX MENTAL HEALTH NEEDS OR WHO ARE NEURODIVERGENT

As far back as 20 years ago it was identified that university students were at specific risk of developing mental health problems and it was estimated that

29% of students had an identifiable mental health issue.[22] Undoubtably, you will have several tutees with mental health issues. These issues might vary in complexity and could include anxiety, psychosis, and bipolar disorder.[23] Some students will come to university with a diagnosis; others might receive one while also struggling with studies and university life. You may feel anxious yourself about supporting a student with such issues, but your role is the same as supporting students without these issues. You are not a counsellor and if the student needs expert intervention they should be referred to the relevant service.

Referral is key in supporting students if they need that expert assistance, but so is keeping in contact with them and managing their expectations. All students, but particularly those struggling with their mental health or who are not 'neuro-typical,' for example students with ADHD, or who are on the autistic spectrum, need to have clear information about what support they can receive from you and from central services. It is extremely important to set this out at the beginning of the year in your first meetings with students, so they do not feel abandoned and let down by you. Students with these complex issues or students who have been involved with state services often find it difficult to build trust and can feel neglected and betrayed if you are not clear at the outset what support you will provide and what support someone else might give.

Hopefully, students who come to university with a diagnosis will have support plans in place, but very often students will not have been diagnosed or will need referring to local services. This is when it is crucial to know about your university's support services. You will need the tutee's written consent to a referral, or you may have a self-referral mechanism or both. The student should be actively involved in any referral: what do they want/need help with, do they want support? Only by discussing this can you refer to the appropriate team. Once you have referred them to counselling services or the disability team, arrange a follow up meeting to check they are in the system, they have been seen by the support team, and that this support is working for them. This is what is meant by active referral: continuing to offer subsidiary support to the student while experts give specific advice and support.

---

[22] See studentminds.org.uk/uploads/3/7/8/4/3784584/grand_challenges_report_for_public.pdf (accessed 3 October 2023).
[23] See ucas.com/file/513961/download?token=wAaKRniC (accessed 3 October 2023).

11.7.1 Case Study

Two students, one already diagnosed and receiving support, the other not diagnosed but receiving some intermittent assistance, came seeking personal tutoring support for different reasons. The first diagnosed student had a myriad of support for complex psychiatric needs and was already in the health care system.

This student needed reassuring that they were able to complete their studies and that their health issues were not a bar to this. They needed practical advice regarding accommodation, where central support services were able to assist, and support regarding resit and study breaks. This student needed a listening supportive ear, a safe place to come and discuss academic issues and to feel they would be accepted and not judged. They did not require any special expertise: they simply needed a personal tutor who was available to discuss academic and practical concerns and help with time management. Again, the VESPA toolkit was helpful in relation to organisational and time management tools. This student also felt supported by being able to attend drop-in sessions, but due to their high-risk status we also checked in with them every fortnight if we had not had contact.

The other student, although much lower risk, needed more intensive intervention as they had not been diagnosed and needed to access specialist support. This student was managing academically but was struggling generally with their mental health, which had impacted on their grades and ability to meet deadlines. The student was receiving intermittent support externally, but felt they needed additional support. They were referred to the university wellbeing services, but due to the high number of students with such issues was on a waiting list, and as such relied more heavily on personal tutors for support and reassurance. We could not provide counselling, but we could provide an empathetic ear and offer practical support including signposting to other services, such as learner support and disability services to get ahead in relation to any potential personal learning plan. This student also required advice about how to apply for extensions but the most supportive thing we did for this student was again to be available during drop-in sessions to listen to their concerns and to chase up referrals.

Students may not reach their full potential for many reasons, but being neuro-divergent or struggling with mental health issues should not be two of them.

11.8 GOOD PRACTICE WHEN DEALING WITH 'COMMUTER STUDENTS', THOSE STRUGGLING WITH LONELINESS AND LACK OF BELONGING, AND STUDENTS NEW TO HE

At Manchester Met, we have a large proportion of students who, rather than finishing A levels and moving away to study at university, study with us as this is their home institution. There are various reasons why students choose to do this, but many of these 'commuter' students are not your 'traditional' students. Some of your tutees may have chosen to study close to home due to financial reasons; others may have caring responsibilities; for others it may be cultural reasons: they will all have a different university experience and student journey than those who have moved away. Due to this many of these students struggle to fit in and feel they don't belong. Helping students celebrate their own identity and find likeminded people is often key to ensuring your tutees have a great student experience; showcasing opportunities for this and ensuring students are aware of the sheer volume of opportunities should be a priority when you meet new students for the first time. It is important students find their 'tribe' so they can feel validated, and this may be the first opportunity for some of your tutees to be able to do this.

There are some excellent resources to help students make the transition from school or college to university. One such resource is from Student Minds, the UK's leading student mental health charity,[24] which provides a transitions guide. Your own university is also likely to have guides for students about what to expect; there will be induction activities and students should be directed to the Student Union, central services and the student law society for guidance and support. The one common thing I think all these tutees (and possibly all students and all of us), have in common is the fear of being judged: judged for not being good enough, judged for being weak enough to succumb to a mental health issue, judged for not fitting in. One key attribute we must all have as personal tutors is to be non-judgemental, this is clearly crucial to building an effective relationship with all your tutees, but even more so with those who may feel they don't belong.

Students who have non-traditional backgrounds and those who commute sometimes feel they do not get the full university experience and that they are missing out on opportunities due to other commitments or financial constraints. Some students will come and seek you out to discuss what they can do to improve their job prospects, but others may feel unable to speak out about a lack of access to schemes or the fact they feel like the only student not living

---

[24] See studentminds.org.uk/ (accessed 3 October 2023).

in halls. Issues may only be discussed when they have almost given up on their student experience.

11.8.1 Case Study

One such student came to light due to lack of attendance at sessions, they had been passing assessments and keeping up with work but had started to fall behind. They were therefore contacted by their personal tutor to check on their welfare. The student was firstly almost overwhelmed that someone cared about their wellbeing, but also then felt enabled to discuss what had been causing the non-attendance. Something as simple as this short 'checking in' email is sometimes sufficient to get the student to open up. This student commuted in from home, was from an 'atypical' student background and had found it difficult to make friends as they felt they had nothing in common with other students, they said they felt alone and lonely. Paradoxically this is one of the most common issues I see as a personal tutor, particularly post COVID-19:[25] tutees often struggle to connect with others, feel uncomfortable in class as they feel excluded, and gradually attend less often.

With this student we offered guidance regarding opportunities to make connections and used confidence building and resilience resources from our central resources. We gave a lot of information about societies, free activities, and 'pop-up' events happening on campus, such as free sports sessions and coffee and cake sessions with our student experience officers. In addition, it was sometimes possible to get several tutees to come to the same drop-in session which could spark a connection. An important aspect of dealing with this issue for this student was to show the student this was not an unusual issue, and they would not be judged because they were lonely.

Another commuter student with caring and employment commitments came to speak to us about gaining legal work experience. They had found it extremely difficult to take up opportunities because of these commitments: they were unable to find alternative carers or change work shifts unless they had a great deal of notice. This student needed practical help to look at viable work experience options: with the help of one of our employability teams the student was able to secure work experience. Only by discussing this in detail with the student did we appreciate their restrictions.

---

[25] See studentminds.org.uk/student-mental-health-in-a-pandemic.html (accessed 3 October 2023).

11.9 CONCLUSION

Effective tutoring is active listening, effective referral and following up with the student to ensure they have played an active role in resolving their issue. There is no magic trick to being an effective personal tutor, it isn't a 'lost or elusive art,'[26] it is a pivotal part of the student experience and getting this role right can make or break the student journey. Recent research has found that the ability to communicate effectively is the crucial skill required to perform this role well.[27] It is important to care about students, to really listen to them and to want to support them on their learning journey,[28] other attributes are all secondary to this. If you do not label students, use your central resources, and refer and check in on your students, you will be effective in this role.

Key things to ensure you are providing an inclusive provision are:

- Get the lines of communication right. Listen without judgement or interruption so the student can be really heard. Don't be afraid of silence: students often need a little time to open up.
- Make personal tutoring relevant to your individual tutees.
- Discuss what they wish to focus on, then empower students to bring about the changes they want.
- Establish and manage expectations (both in relation to your expertise and time). Ensure students are aware other people will be involved in their learning journey, not just you.
- Build trust: by being true to your word and managing expectations, only then will students feel able to bring all their concerns to you.
- You are not alone! Ensure you check what central resources and support services your institution has and make use of these.

---

[26] Emily McIntosh and David Grey, *Career advice: how to be an effective personal tutor* (2017), available at: timeshighereducation.com/news/career-advice-how-to-be-an-effective-personal-tutor (accessed 3 October 2023).
[27] Craig M. McGill, Mehvash Ali and Dionne Barton, 'Skills and Competencies for Effective Academic Advising and Personal Tutoring' (2020) 5 Frontiers in Educ.
[28] Ibid.

Index

academic support
    pastoral support, and 40, 55–7
academics
    racial diversity 106
    role of 27, 48–9
    supporting support officers 67–8
active listening 160
active referral 160
Advance HE Education for Mental Health Toolkit 141
advertising available support 72
ambition 18
anxiety
anti-racist pedagogy 102
    see also race
anti-racist space in classrooms 112–18
    case study: Philip 36–7
approachability 66–7, 129–30
assessment
    role of 130–32
    wellbeing integration into classroom 149
assurance 28
asynchronous/synchronous support 97–8
authenticity
    encouraging others 21
    generally 19–20
    introducing yourself 21
    sharing experiences 20–1
    student support work 22

BAME (Black, Asian and minority ethnic) 103
barriers to engagement
    sitting behind desk 151
barriers to support
    competition amongst students 52–3
    scheduling sessions 51–2
    students reaching out 50–52
    understanding barriers 41–3
    waiting lists for services 53–4

belonging
    importance of 3
    lack of 169–70
    meaning of pastoral support 42
bereavement 60, 79, 81
BME (Black and minority ethnic) 103
body language 137–8
boundaries
    limitations of role 2, 70–72
    work/life boundaries 69–70

CADSIF formula 27–9
care
    meaning of pastoral support 40
carers, students who are 162–4
case studies
    Christine 31–4
    exercise 37–8
    Philip 36–7
    Samir 29–31
    Winnie 34–5
challenges faced by ECRs *see* early career researchers
change
    embracing 22
    long-term changes 125
    noticing as aid to change 138
classroom interaction 132–3
classroom, pastoral support in 43
classroom, wellbeing in
    approachability 129–30
    assessment, role of 130–32
    conclusions 139
    confidentiality
        classroom teaching 123–5
        escalating confidential information 121–2
        generally 121
        impact on lesson plans and module aims 124–5

impact on student participation
123–4
long-term changes 125
reflective practice 125
feedback, role of 130–32
inclusivity
inclusive design and delivery
127–9
student wellbeing 126
introduction 120–21
noticing
aid to change 138
body language 137–8
classroom interaction 132–3
fictional scenario 133–7
meaning 132
collaboration
student peer relationships 53
support officer/academic
relationships 68–9
with colleagues 3, 9, 23
with students 12–13, 23
colonialism 109
colour-blindness 118
communication
personal tutors 160
support officer/academic
relationships 67–8, 72–3
community
distance learning 97
importance of 3
pastoral support 40–42, 45, 53
staff 3
Community Hub 12
commuter students 169–70
compassion 11
competition amongst students 52–3
complex mental health needs 166–8
confidence, lack of 164–6
confidentiality
classroom teaching 123–5
escalating confidential information
121–2
generally 121
impact on lesson plans and module
aims 124–5
impact on student participation
123–4
long-term changes 125
reflective practice 125

contact with student 28
content of curriculum 146–7
conversations
power of 19
race 103–4, 110–12
course design
inclusivity and 125, 127–9
Covid-19 pandemic 26
criminality 121
curriculum, integration of wellbeing into
case study: contract law 152–4
conclusions 156
curriculum content 146–7
curriculum delivery 150–52
curriculum design 147–50
importance of wellbeing within
curriculum 143–5
integration at module level 155–6
integration at programme level
154–5, 156
introduction 140–3
methods of integration 145–52
wellbeing checklist 155–6

data protection 122
deficit model 3
delivery of curriculum 150–52
design of curriculum 147–50
dialogue 28
digital poverty 99
disabilities
accessing support 60–61, 63, 65
uniting characteristics 81–2
distance learning
challenges 97–100
community building 97
conclusion 100
digital poverty 99
forums 95–7
introduction 88–9
monitoring student progress 99
Open University 89
pastoral support 89–90
peer mentoring 92–4
relationship building 92
role of tutors 91–2
student support teams 91
summary 101
synchronous/asynchronous support
97–8

teamworking 90–92
diverse student body 2, 157–8

early career researchers
    challenges faced by 78–82
    emergency situations 81
    end of lesson chats 79
    flown in ECRs 74, 78
    home grown ECRs 74, 76, 78
    inappropriate comments in class 79–80
    kinship events 74, 77, 87
    reflective events 74, 77, 87
    sidestep ECRs 74, 76, 78
    strategies to manage expectations
        acknowledging and accepting role 86–7
        evidence trail of work undertaken 85–6
        formal mentorship structure 84–5
        resource bank 83–4
        techniques for anticipation and deflection 85
    summary 87
    trigger events 74, 77, 87
    uniting characteristics 81–2, 87
emergency situations 81
end of lesson chats 79
ethnicity
    uniting characteristics 81–2

fear of failure 52, 130
fear of missing out 13
feedback
    role of 130–32
    safety via feedback 117–18
fictional personas 26–7
financial hardship 61–2, 121
finding your people *see* networks
flown in early career researchers 74, 78
follow-ups 29, 69, 70, 73
forums
    distance learning 95–7

gender
    see also sex and gender
    leadership role 8
getting to know students 26–9
glory/housekeeping work 76, 77, 78

hierarchies
    generally 17–18
    maintaining ambitions 18
    power of conversation 19
    support from other leaders 18–19
holistic approach
    CADSIF formula 27–9
    case study: Christine 31–4
    case study: exercise 37–8
    case study: Philip 36–7
    case study: Samir 29–31
    case study: Winnie 34–5
    getting to know students 26–9
    holistic approach 26
    introduction 24–5
    key questions 26
    reflecting on past experience 25
    role of legal academic 27
    summary 38
home grown early career researchers 74, 76, 78
home life pressures
    case study: Christine 31–4
housekeeping/glory work 76, 77, 78
humanity 11

imperialism 109
imposter syndrome 2, 6, 20, 23, 64, 143, 164–6
inability to assist 71–2
inclusive spaces 106
inclusivity
    generally 3
    inclusive design and delivery 127–9
    personal tutors 159
    student wellbeing 126
individuality 14
inequality 103–4
information provision 29
interdisciplinary approach 9
international students 62–3

kinship conversations 81
kinship events 74, 77, 87
kitchen-sink approach 8

language
    international students 62–3
    pastoral support 44

Index

leadership
    authenticity 19–22
    being realistic about capabilities 13–15
    finding your people 15–17
    introduction 5–7
    practicing what we preach 7–13
    summary 22–3
    unhealthy hierarchies 17–19
learning difficulties 121
legal academics *see* academics
LGBTQ+ 81, 82
life events
    uniting characteristics 81–2
limitations of role 70–72
listening, active 160
local authority prior involvement 160–62
loneliness 29, 34, 52, 169–70

mental health
    Advance HE Education for Mental Health Toolkit 141
    confidentiality 121
    stigmas 44
    support officers' role 60–1
    waiting lists 53
mentorship structures 84–5

named roles
    pastoral support 43–4
networks
    creating new networks 16–17
    generally 15
    off-campus connections 15
    putting yourself out there 16
neurodiversity 61, 121, 166–8
non-attendance
    pastoral support 42–3
noticing
    aid to change 138
    body language 137–8
    classroom interaction 132–3
    fictional scenario 133–7
    meaning 132
nurturing teacher 151

off-campus connections 15
Office for Students 142
online learning *see* distance learning

open access
    distance learning 89
Open University *see* distance learning
outside interests 9–11

parental pressures
    case study: Winnie 34–5
parents, students who are 162–4
peer mentoring
    distance learning 92–4
personal tutors
    active listening 160
    active referral 160
    carers, students who are 162–4
    changing student cohort 157–8
    commuter students 169–70
    complex mental health needs 166–8
    conclusions 171
    good communication 160
    good practice 160–70
    imposter syndrome 164–6
    inclusivity 159
    lack of belonging 169–70
    lack of confidence 164–6
    loneliness 169–70
    neurodiversity 166–8
    new HE students 169–70
    parents, students who are 162–4
    prior involvement of student with local authorities or other services 160–62
    role of 158
    variation in approach 2
personalised approach
    diversity of student body 3
    effective pastoral support 45–8
    meaning of pastoral support 40–42, 45
personas 26–7
physical health
    support officers' role 60
postgraduate students 2
problem-based learning 148–9
progress of student
    confidentiality 121
    distance learning 99
putting yourself out there 16

race
    academic staff 106

anti-racist approaches 106–7, 110
BAME 103
BME 103
colonialism 109
colour-blindness 118
conversations about race 103–4, 110–12
creating anti-racist space in classrooms 112–18
environments of enquiry and interest 113–14
imperialism 109
inclusive spaces 106
inequality 103–4
introduction 102–3
law education in England and Wales 104–7
legislation 109
personal tax 107–8
safety norms 114–15
safety via feedback 117–18
showing vulnerability 115–16
suggested actions 118–19
terminology 103
referral, active 160
reflection
   confidentiality 125
   past experience 23, 25
   reflective events 74, 77, 87
relationship building
   distance learning 92
   pastoral support 41, 42, 49, 52
reluctance to ask for help 64–5
resource bank 83–4

safety norms 114–15
safety via feedback 117–18
self-care 7–13
   collaboration with colleagues 9
   collaboration with students 12–13
   compassion 11
   generally 7–8
   humanity 11
   outside interests 9–11
Self-Determination Theory 72
settling into student life
   case study: Samir 29–31
sex and gender
   see also early career researchers

   disparities in legal academic environment 74–6
   formal pastoral support 76–8
   housekeeping/glory work 76, 77, 78
   informal pastoral support 76–8
   introduction 74
   legal profession statistics 75
   pay gap 75
   work-life balance 87
   York Law School 76–8
sexual assaults 61
sexual behaviour 82
sexuality
   uniting characteristics 81–2
sharing experiences 20–1, 47
sidestep early career researchers 74, 76, 78
signposting 28–9, 48
social media
   safeguarding support groups 96–7
Socratic method 151
space to speak 41
statistics
   racial diversity 104–5
   sex and gender 75
student support leadership *see* leadership
student support pathways *see* holistic approach
student views of pastoral support
   academic support, and 55–7
   barriers 50–54
   conclusion 57
   effectiveness 45–8
   introduction 39
   meaning 40–45
   role of academics 48–9
   summary 57–8
substance abuse 121
support officers
   approachability 66–7
   collaboration 68–9
   common wellbeing issues 60–62
   inability to assist 71–2
   international students 62–3
   introduction 59
   law students or students in general 63–4
   limitations of role 70–72
   preference to approaching tutors 65–6

reluctance to ask for help 64–5
summary 72–3
support from academics 67–8
work/life boundaries 69–70
student support teams
    distance learning 91
surveys 14
synchronous/asynchronous support 97–8

teamworking
    distance learning 90–92
time constraints 3
    limitations of support officer role 70–72
trigger events 74, 77, 87

unhealthy hierarchies
    generally 17–18
    maintaining ambitions 18
    power of conversation 19
    support from other leaders 18–19
uniting characteristics 81–2

VESPA Mindset Workbook 165, 168
virtual learning environments 89
vulnerability 115–16

Windrush scandal 107–8
work/life balance 1, 69–70
workload
    generally 13–14
    individuality 14
    realism 22
    respecting others' realities 14–15